T0354664

CROSSROADS

Seeking God to Discern Next Steps: A Forty-Day Devotional

RYAN STRATTON

WESTBOW
PRESS®
A DIVISION OF THOMAS NELSON
& ZONDERVAN

WestBow Press books may be ordered through booksellers or by contacting:

WestBow Press
A Division of Thomas Nelson & Zondervan
1663 Liberty Drive
Bloomington, IN 47403
www.westbowpress.com
844-714-3454

All scripture quotations are taken from The Holy Bible, New
International Version®, NIV® Copyright © 1973, 1978, 1984, 2011 by
Biblica, Inc.® Used by permission. All rights reserved worldwide.

ISBN: 978-1-6642-8985-7 (sc)
ISBN: 978-1-6642-8986-4 (hc)
ISBN: 978-1-6642-8987-1 (e)

Library of Congress Control Number: 2023901783

Print information available on the last page.

WestBow Press rev. date: 01/31/2023

To my beautiful wife and children, who
always seek God's direction

And for those who seek God's guidance and direction in their lives

God does not exist to answer our prayers, but by
our prayers we come to discern the mind of God.
—Oswald Chambers

PREFACE

A few years ago, I was in a personal crisis and needed to make some decisions. I had several options available, but I found myself thinking too much about the options that lay ahead of me. These decisions were overwhelming me. I was thankful that I was about to be on a spiritual Sabbath retreat. At the beginning of this spiritual Sabbath retreat with some close friends, I decided to go for a walk by myself and pray. During that walk, I began to realize that we end up asking the wrong questions when we make decisions. I'll speak about this in the introduction.

Since that retreat, I have thought more and more about how we make decisions and what we can do to put ourselves in the position to hear God more clearly. This has not been an easy task because I want to make the change here and now. It is challenging to *wait* for the direction to be uncovered.

For some time I have wanted to write about something that Elijah and Elisha went through in their lives. I felt this was the time to do that. Starting on day 4, we'll begin with 1 Kings 17 and go all the way through 2 Kings 2:22.

This devotional book is a culmination of the thinking and praying I have been doing over the past few years. My hope and prayer is that you will find comfort in knowing that God is with you and that God is guiding you.

May we always have the ears and hearts to hear and experience the presence of the living and speaking God, who is with us always.

ACKNOWLEDGMENTS

I am forever grateful for my wife, Amanda. She is a person of deep faith and is an inspiration to me daily. My love for her grows each and every day.

I also am grateful for my four children, who are a constant reminder of God's grace and provision, and for the churches I serve as pastor, which allow me time to write and pray, as well as study the scriptures to preach each week.

I am grateful for my parents, who always have been encouraging to me and who allow me to talk things out, no matter how old I am.

Finally, I am incredibly grateful for my friends, with whom I get to go on the Sabbath retreats. Shook, Rusty, Dave, Adam, Brock—you all (and so many more) have been influences on my life more than you may know. For that, I give God thanks that I know you guys.

INTRODUCTION

What are you hoping to do next? What choices do you have to make? How will you make these decisions and be at peace with your choices?

These are questions we face, but there comes a time when we need to make decisions, and that task can be daunting and overwhelming. We can feel as if we're at a crossroads, trying to figure out in which direction to go.

How do we know which way to go? What if we have been looking at the decision-making process all wrong? What if we've not been asking the right questions?

Most of us have been at a crossroads and have had to figure out which path will be the best for our lives. Some of the questions we may ask are:

- Which way does God want me to go?
- How do I know if I've made the right choice?
- What is the best option for me right now?
- What if this is not the best option in the future?

If you don't believe in God, the question of what he thinks will not enter your thought process. Regardless, here's the deal: I think we are asking the wrong questions.

A few years ago, I came to a crossroads and felt that I needed to make a decision. It was weighing on me because I tried to think of every possible angle or outcome that *could* come along. In this process, I felt God say, *Stop and look*. So I looked down and saw four different paths that I could take while on this trail.

What did I do? I studied where the paths went. Of course, I could have just returned the way I'd come, on the fourth path, but it was a surreal moment. It was as if a light bulb went off in my head, and then a wave of peace came over me. It was nice. What was it that happened? It suddenly dawned on me that no matter which path I chose, God would be there, working in and through me.

That's when it hit me! We ask the wrong questions. We often wonder, "Which path should I choose?" but we should ask, "What kind of person I will be (or do I want to be) in whichever decision I make?"

That is an important question. God will work wherever we are and in whatever we decide. Therefore, when we consider which decision will feed our souls and help us become the persons we desire and are meant to be by the grace of God, *that* is the path we should take.

As the Crusader tells Indiana Jones when he's trying to choose the chalice, be sure to choose wisely.

WHAT IS DISCERNMENT?

In his book *Reading the Signs of Daily Life,* Henri Nouwen gives a good understanding of *discernment.* Let's use his words to give a definition:

> Christian discernment is not the same as decision making. Reaching a decision can be straightforward: we consider our goals and options; maybe we list the pros and cons of each possible choice; and then we choose the action that meets our goal most effectively. Discernment, on the other hand, is about listening and responding to that place within us where our deepest desires align with God's desire. As discerning people, we sift through our impulses, motives, and options to discover which ones lead us closer to divine love and compassion for ourselves

and other people and which ones lead us further away.[1]

Discernment reveals new priorities, directions, and gifts from God. We come to realize that what previously seemed so important for our lives loses its power over us. Our desire to be successful, well liked and influential becomes increasingly less important as we move closer to God's heart. To our surprise, we even may experience a strange inner freedom to follow a new call or direction as previous concerns move into the background of our consciousness. We begin to see the beauty of the small and hidden life that Jesus lived in Nazareth. Most rewarding of all is the discovery that as we pray more each day, God's will—that is, God's concrete ways of loving us and our world—gradually is made known to us.[2]

FORTY DAYS OF DISCERNMENT

When Pilate was questioning Jesus, he asked a question for which we all still seek an answer: "What is *truth*?" (John 18:38 NIV, emphasis mine). This is what I hope you are seeking over the next forty days. Now, this is not about seeking any other truth that discounts Jesus. I pray you are fully committed to and framing your life after the truth that Jesus is *the* Kings of kings, Lord of lords, Master of all, your (and the world's) Lord and Savior, and the way, truth, and life.

What will you be undertaking? What are the next steps—plain and simple?

I believe that when we have a decision to make, we come to

---

[1] Henri Nouwen, *Discernment: Reading the Signs of Daily Life* (HarperOne, 2013), loc. 172, Kindle.

[2] Ibid., 17.

a "burning bush" moment (see Exodus 3), where God is trying to get our attention to speak to us. God is saying how we live in relationship with him and how we should move forward with him for his work in the world. The question now shifts from "What is truth?" or "What is it God is asking me to do?" to "How is God calling me to best faithfully serve him and his people in the world?" In other words, "How is God making me to be more like Jesus and be part of his mission in this world?"

I tend to struggle with the patience needed to thoroughly discern (weighing out the best options). I believe that when I hear from God, I can trust I am making the right decision. But when it comes to big decisions that may require significant change, I am not as patient; therefore, I find myself living in a period of anxiety because I want to make a decision and move forward. I'd bet this describes you too, so this is a journey I invite you to take—to listen intently to the voice of God.

God tells Moses, "Take off your sandals, for the place you are standing is holy ground" (Exodus 3:5 NIV). I often tried to explain this as God telling Moses not to bring any "defiled" dirt or the past into his presence (or something like that), but something has made me stop and pay better attention.[3]

We are always ready to move when we're wearing our shoes (sandals). We have somewhere else to be. But God tells Moses, "This is where you need to be." So take off your shoes and listen. Enjoy this moment. Allow the presence of God to change your life and life mission.

That is the purpose of this forty-day journey of discernment. I hope you will do your best to sit still and listen to what God has in mind. Be present and available to the one who is truth and who will lead you to truth.

This is not a journey to ask God to bless any decision we want to

---

[3] A. J. Swoboda, *After Doubt: How to Question Your Faith without Losing It*, (Grand Rapids, MI: Brazos Press, 2021). 124.

make. Instead, this is a journey to empty ourselves of our thoughts, desires, and plans and to submit everything to God (Proverbs 16) to best live into God's calling on our lives. To do this, we need to understand and remember who God says we are.

> "You yourselves have seen what I did to Egypt and how I carried you on eagles' wings and brought you to myself. Now, if you obey me fully and keep my covenant, then out of all nations you will be my treasured possession. Although the whole earth is mine, you will be for me a kingdom of priests and a holy nation." These are the words you are to speak to the Israelites. (Exodus 19:4–6 NIV)

> But you are a chosen people, a royal priesthood, a holy nation, God's special possession, that you may declare the praises of him who called you out of darkness into his wonderful light. Once you were not a people, but now you are the people of God; once you had not received mercy, but now you have received mercy. (1 Peter 2:9–10 NIV)

I know there will be days when you will go into this time kicking and screaming, not wanting to be patient or do the internal work needed. But I am praying God will do his work and bring trust and clarity to your mind and heart.

Let's pray: Gracious and holy God, here I am. I am trusting you for this journey of faith. May I be open to your Word and trust you completely with what you say and what you have in store. I am yours.

WESLEY COVENANT PRAYER

I am no longer my own, but yours.
Put me to what you will,
rank me with whom you will;
put me to doing,
put me to suffering;
let me be employed for you,
or laid aside for you,
exalted for you,
or brought low for you;
let me be full, let me be empty,
let me have all things,
let me have nothing:
I freely and wholeheartedly yield all things
to your pleasure and disposal.
And now, glorious and blessed God,
Father, Son and Holy Spirit,
you are mine and I am yours.
So be it.
And the covenant now made on earth,
let it be ratified in heaven.
Amen.

HOW TO USE THIS DEVOTIONAL RESOURCE

First and foremost, my words throughout this devotional book *do not* replace whatever God speaks to you. Instead, these words, these reflections, are meant to spur your thinking and awareness of who God is and who God says you are and to help you see what God says to do.

This is a journey—a journey of spiritual renewal, reflection, and listening to the voice of God.

During these forty days, we will employ three main spiritual disciplines besides prayer and scripture reading: fasting, solitude, and silence. I love how John Wesley describes spiritual disciplines as means of grace—these are "means" by which we open ourselves to receiving the presence and grace of God through Jesus Christ and empowered by the Holy Spirit.

Choose the best time of day to read the scripture and have some uninterrupted time in prayer. Schedule this time on your phone or another calendar system if you need to.

When we come to a place of discernment, and we're trying to figure out what to do next, it is much too easy to make a quick decision based upon the little information we have that gives us goosebumps. It is also too easy to react to misinformation. These forty days are meant to slow us down so we can enjoy the presence of God and seek his mind and ways.

After all, the life we live truly is a gift from God, so why not spend this time with him to see what he might say? We often think we know what God wants us to do, but we may not spend as much time considering who God wants us to become. That is the main focus of this devotional book.

As you read the scripture, stay as quiet and still as possible. See what the Spirit says through the scripture. Then, use the reflections to help you think through and pray through the scripture for the day. Your journey, beginning on day 4, looks at the life and ministry of Elijah and the beginnings of Elisha's ministry.

Be sure to take notes along the way to remember and track the experience of your journey. At the end of the week, you are invited to reflect on what God has spoken to you throughout the week.

At the end of each day, we'll pray the Wesley Covenant Prayer. This is to make sure we are open to the Holy Spirit's leading and that we're aligning ourselves with God's will. My hope and prayer is that we are genuinely available to the movement of the Holy Spirit, which is all we seek and desire.

FASTING

Plain and simple, fasting is giving up something *physically* so we can hear from heaven *spiritually*. When the days call for fasting, what will we give up? We must sacrifice whatever draws our focus and attention away from God. When we feel tempted to reach for what we've given up, we must tell God we are more interested in his presence than what tempts us at that moment (food, television, anything).

SILENCE

Our world is filled with too much noise. We do not always have enough silence in our lives. We must try to block out the noise of the world around us so we can hear better with our hearts. At first, silence will feel uncomfortable because it's hard to have everything else silent besides our minds. Then, silence will be like an enemy because we will be tempted to fill the space with noise. Finally, silence becomes a friend. It is in this space we can better hear the voice of God that we so easily drown out the other noise throughout the day.

SOLITUDE

It can be uncomfortable to be alone or to find time to be in solitude. But this practice will force us to pay more attention to the presence of God, rather than to anything or anyone else around us. We can create a prayer closet or find a space that can be ours and ours alone at whatever time of day we go through this devotional and discernment process.

I am praying for you. Although this may not be an easy journey, you can be assured that God is with you and is guiding you to become the person he wants you to be especially in this time of discerning whatever decision you need to make.

Ultimately, the decision you're in the process of making *must* be made for the glory of God. Anything else will mean that you may have been too haphazard in your decision-making and have missed out on some essential things you needed to do.

Before we begin this process, let's take time to invite the presence and Spirit of God to guide and lead us as he makes himself known and helps to illuminate the paths we should take.

LITURGY FOR GUIDANCE AND DIRECTION[4]

Opening
Leader: Thy Word is a lamp unto my feet.
People: And light unto my path.

Scripture
The Lord is my shepherd, I lack nothing.
He makes me lie down in green pastures,
he leads me beside quiet waters,
he refreshes my soul.
He guides me along the right paths
for his name's sake.
Even though I walk
through the darkest valley,
I will fear no evil,
for you are with me;
your rod and your staff,
they comfort me.

---

[4] Winfield Bevins, *Living Room Liturgy* (Franklin, TN: Seedbed Publishing, 2020), 31–32.

You prepare a table before me
in the presence of my enemies.
You anoint my head with oil;
my cup overflows.
Surely your goodness and love will follow me
all the days of my life,
and I will dwell in the house of the LORD
forever. (Ps. 23)

Leader: The Word of the Lord.
People: Thanks be to God.

Prayer
Leader: The Lord be with you.
People: And also with you.

Leader: Let us pray. Heavenly Father, in you we live and move and have our being. When the way is dark and we cannot see the road ahead, we humbly pray you guide and govern us by your Holy Spirit, that in all the cares and occupations of our life we may not forget you, but may remember that we are ever walking in your sight; through Jesus Christ our Lord. Amen.

Reflection
At this time, you may take a few minutes for a short reflection or personal prayer that goes along with the theme of the day.

The Lord's Prayer
Our Father, who art in heaven,
hallowed be thy name.
Thy kingdom come,

thy will be done on earth as it is in heaven.
Give us this day our daily bread.
And forgive us our trespasses,
as we forgive those who trespass against us.
And lead us not into temptation,
but deliver us from evil.
For thine is the kingdom,
and the power,
and the glory, forever. Amen.

Closing
Leader: Let us bless the Lord who guides our paths.
People: Thanks be to God.

Then Jesus was led by the Spirit into the wilderness to be tempted by the devil. After fasting forty days and forty nights, he was hungry. The tempter came to him and said, "If you are the Son of God, tell these stones to become bread." Jesus answered, "It is written: 'Man shall not live on bread alone, but on every word that comes from the mouth of God.'" Then the devil took him to the holy city and had him stand on the highest point of the temple. "If you are the Son of God," he said, "throw yourself down. For it is written: "'He will command his angels concerning you, and they will lift you up in their hands, so that you will not strike your foot against a stone.'" Jesus answered him, "It is also written: 'Do not put the Lord your God to the test.'" Again, the devil took him to a very high mountain and showed him all the kingdoms of the world and their splendor. "All this I will give you," he said, "if you will bow down and worship me." Jesus said to him, "Away from me, Satan! For it is written: 'Worship the Lord your God, and serve him only.'" Then the devil left him, and angels came and attended him." (Matthew 4:1–11 NIV)

You may not feel like you have been *led* into this discerning experience. It may feel more like you have been *thrust* into it. But also realize it's important to do this process more often. You always need to discern God's will and direction for your life.

We may need to realize that God may not be calling us to change directions completely. Nevertheless, we have a great opportunity ahead to hear from God. This is a journey to see how God calls us into a more trustful life—trusting in him, the saving work of Jesus, and the enabling empowerment of the Holy Spirit.

I've thought about where to begin, and I believe the best place is in Matthew's account of Jesus's temptations in the wilderness. We do this journey over forty days because Moses, Elijah, and Jesus all took forty days to listen to the voice and heart of God. We may think we know the answer and may not want to embark on this faith journey. This is a time of wrestling with God. Like Jacob, in Genesis 32:22–32, I am praying and asking God to bless this time.

You also may be like Jacob, in that you have difficulty knowing you can trust God with this decision. You may feel that you have to make God do what you want to do.

But look at Jesus's temptation, and pay attention to Jesus's unswerving dedication, hope, and trust in God's direction and purpose. I am praying for you to have this for yourself.

You may be tempted to make things happen yourself. You may have a knee-jerk reaction, yet Jesus reminds Satan and us that God will provide what we need. God's voice, God's Word, is what we need to live and thrive in this life.

Look at the temptation to put God to the test. This means we try to do something careless to see that God is who he says he is and that he will do what he says he will do. Instead of living haphazardly, we should take intentional steps to follow the one who is leading.

Finally, the temptation is to make our lives as comfortable as possible. This would mean bowing down to the false gods of success, comfort, fame, riches, and so forth. We are called to be faithful to the rightful ruler of the universe. We can try to place ourselves as rulers, but that would mean we put ourselves in the position of God.

The underlying assumption for all of this boils down to the word *trust*. Do you trust God with everything? Or do you trust yourself more than God?

Let's pray: Lord Jesus, guide me, and reveal yourself and your direction to me.

WESLEY COVENANT PRAYER

I am no longer my own, but yours.
Put me to what you will,
rank me with whom you will;
put me to doing,
put me to suffering;
let me be employed for you,
or laid aside for you,
exalted for you,
or brought low for you;
let me be full, let me be empty,
let me have all things,
let me have nothing:
I freely and wholeheartedly yield all things
to your pleasure and disposal.
And now, glorious and blessed God,
Father, Son and Holy Spirit,
you are mine and I am yours.
So be it.
And the covenant now made on earth,
let it be ratified in heaven.
Amen.

DAILY REFLECTION

Write about how you experienced God today and what God said to you. How is it with your soul regarding the choice(s) ahead of you?

> Rejoice always, pray continually, give thanks in all circumstances; for this is God's will for you in Christ Jesus. Do not quench the Spirit. Do not treat prophecies with contempt but test them all; hold on to what is good, reject every kind of evil. May God himself, the God of peace, sanctify you through and through. May your whole spirit, soul and body be kept blameless at the coming of our Lord Jesus Christ. The one who calls you is faithful, and he will do it. (1 Thessalonians5:16–24 NIV)

After reading this passage, do you realize how much *joy* there is in being in this position of discernment? Why? Because you can trust that God is with you and is guiding you. No matter how much you get bogged down in the grind of thinking, *I need to go in a certain direction*, your options are not the real choices.

The real choice is knowing the presence of God, who is leading and working in and through you. The goal is not a destination or making the "right choice." No, the goal is being transformed into the person you have been created to be. The question is not which path to take; the question is, "Who do I want to become?"

You can give thanks in all circumstances because God is changing and leading. You can trust that God is with you and will do what he desires, no matter the decision you have to make. This should be freeing.

But is it?

The truth is, a level of anxiety is challenging to shake. Why? Because you want and need to make the best decision. So even though you are "rejoicing always, praying continually, and giving thanks in all circumstances," you still have a decision to make.

What do you do? Test the Spirit. Check your motives. Seek the face of God. Look for the most loving decision for you, your family, and the mission God has entrusted to you. You test to make sure you are listening to the voice of the living God and that you're not being swayed in any direction that would transform you into a person you do not want to become.

Therefore, seek God to "sanctify you through and through" (making you holy, complete, whole) to be the person to best serve and love God and his people in this life.

Challenge: Fast from dinner.

Pray: Lord, I am hungry, but I am hungrier for you to fill me with what you desire. Fill me with your presence and Spirit, and I will be satisfied.

Let's pray: Lord Jesus, guide me, and reveal yourself and your direction to me.

WESLEY COVENANT PRAYER

I am no longer my own, but yours.
Put me to what you will,
rank me with whom you will;
put me to doing,
put me to suffering;
let me be employed for you,
or laid aside for you,
exalted for you,
or brought low for you;
let me be full, let me be empty,
let me have all things,
let me have nothing:
I freely and wholeheartedly yield all things
to your pleasure and disposal.

And now, glorious and blessed God,
Father, Son and Holy Spirit,
you are mine and I am yours.
So be it.
And the covenant now made on earth,
let it be ratified in heaven.
Amen.

DAILY REFLECTION

Write about how you experienced God today and what God said to you. How is it with your soul regarding the choice(s) ahead of you?

The Lord is my shepherd, I lack nothing. He makes me lie down in green pastures, he leads me beside quiet waters, he refreshes my soul. He guides me along the right paths for his name's sake. Even though I walk through the darkest valley, I will fear no evil, for you are with me; your rod and your staff, they comfort me. You prepare a table before me in the presence of my enemies. You anoint my head with oil; my cup overflows. Surely your goodness and love will follow me all the days of my life, and I will dwell in the house of the Lord forever. (Psalm 23:1–6 NIV)

It can be too easy to be consumed with what we need to decide. Remember it is not about what we do but about who will we become. That question leads to the essential task of seeking God—and God alone.

Psalm 23 reminds us we have everything we need because of God. We lack nothing. We have been given every spiritual blessing under heaven (Ephesians 1), and we have all of this because of the God who is with us, the God we are seeking.

God will work everything together "for the good for those who love him who are called according to his purposes" (Romans 8:28). At the same time, we also need to be vigilant in resting in the presence and Word of God. Why? Because this is where we will find rest; we will find our purpose.

He makes me lie down in green pastures
He leads me beside still waters

He guides me along the right paths for his name's sake

The presence of God brings rest, completeness, and peace. Trusting in God and who God truly is means that our souls are at rest, and we can allow him to lead. These issues come in when we doubt the direction. You may believe you know where to go, but you may be anxious about taking the steps. With God, we are led to the calmness, peace, love, hope, and joy that God brings.

That's the focus—the peace and presence of God. Let go and relax in God's presence. There will be shadows and hard times, but God is with us and is protecting us.

> Even though I walk through the darkest valley, I
> will fear no evil
> For you are with me; your rod and your staff, they
> comfort me
> You prepare a table before me in the presence of my
> enemies,
> You anoint my head with oil; my cup overflows.

Yes, God is present and is doing all of this. He wants his people to trust him and to be led according to his calling and purpose. Of course, not everyone will agree with what needs to be done, but we have nothing to fear because God is with us. We will, one day, get to watch God bring about his complete will. And we will also see that God has been with us this entire time, making us into the people we were created to be.

> Surely your goodness and love will follow [pursue]
> me all the days of my life,
> And I will dwell in the house of the Lord forever.

Let's pray: Lord Jesus, guide me, and reveal yourself and your direction to me.

WESLEY COVENANT PRAYER

I am no longer my own, but yours.
Put me to what you will,
rank me with whom you will;
put me to doing,
put me to suffering;
let me be employed for you,
or laid aside for you,
exalted for you,
or brought low for you;
let me be full, let me be empty,
let me have all things,
let me have nothing:
I freely and wholeheartedly yield all things
to your pleasure and disposal.
And now, glorious and blessed God,
Father, Son and Holy Spirit,
you are mine and I am yours.
So be it.
And the covenant now made on earth,
let it be ratified in heaven. Amen.

DAILY REFLECTION

Write about how you experienced God today and what God said to you. How is it with your soul regarding the choice(s) ahead of you?

Now Elijah the Tishbite, from Tishbe in Gilead, said to Ahab, "As the Lord, the God of Israel, lives, whom I serve, there will be neither dew nor rain in the next few years except at my word." Then the word of the Lord came to Elijah: "Leave here, turn eastward and hide in the Kerith Ravine, east of the Jordan. You will drink from the brook, and I have directed the ravens to supply you with food there." So he did what the Lord had told him. He went to the Kerith Ravine, east of the Jordan, and stayed there. The ravens brought him bread and meat in the morning and bread and meat in the evening, and he drank from the brook." (1 Kings 17:1–6 NIV)

One of the constant challenges is that we can worry about how or if God will provide; we need to know this. (I know he provides; God has provided for my family time and time again.) How will the Holy Spirit move through us to so that we will become the people we need to be to best fulfill our purpose in the ministry to which we're called?

This passage speaks about peace and provision, especially in conflict and adversity. The conflict may be the decision of where God is leading us. The conflict for Elijah came from being the proclaimer of the drought.

God already had provision for Elijah to be nurtured and cared for. Elijah needed to step out in faith and move to where God was leading. How do we know where God is leading? Psalm 119 reminds us God's Word is a lamp unto our feet and a light for our paths. If we follow God's Word, we'll know where to go.

Jesus gave the example in John 5, saying he only does what he sees the Father doing. Where God is working, he will provide. He already has a plan in place for your provision and care. The question now is, will you step out in faith?

Will you hear God, who is speaking clearly?

Will you receive all that God has planned for you?

Let's pray: Lord Jesus, guide me, and reveal yourself and your direction to me.

WESLEY COVENANT PRAYER

I am no longer my own, but yours.
Put me to what you will,
rank me with whom you will;
put me to doing,
put me to suffering;
let me be employed for you,
or laid aside for you,
exalted for you,
or brought low for you;
let me be full, let me be empty,
let me have all things,
let me have nothing:
I freely and wholeheartedly yield all things
to your pleasure and disposal.
And now, glorious and blessed God,
Father, Son and Holy Spirit,
you are mine and I am yours.
So be it.
And the covenant now made on earth,
let it be ratified in heaven.
Amen.

DAILY REFLECTION

Write about how you experienced God today and what God said to you. How is it with your soul regarding the choice(s) ahead of you?

Some time later the brook dried up because there had been no rain in the land. Then the word of the Lord came to him: "Go at once to Zarephath in the region of Sidon and stay there. I have directed a widow there to supply you with food." So he went to Zarephath. When he came to the town gate, a widow was there gathering sticks. He called to her and asked, "Would you bring me a little water in a jar so I may have a drink?" As she was going to get it, he called, "And bring me, please, a piece of bread." "As surely as the Lord your God lives," she replied, "I don't have any bread—only a handful of flour in a jar and a little olive oil in a jug. I am gathering a few sticks to take home and make a meal for myself and my son, that we may eat it—and die." Elijah said to her, "Don't be afraid. Go home and do as you have said. But first make a small loaf of bread for me from what you have and bring it to me, and then make something for yourself and your son. For this is what the Lord, the God of Israel, says: 'The jar of flour will not be used up and the jug of oil will not run dry until the day the Lord sends rain on the land.' She went away and did as Elijah had told her. So there was food every day for Elijah and for the woman and her family. For the jar of flour was not used up and the jug of oil did not run dry, in keeping with the word of the Lord spoken by Elijah. (1 Kings 17:7–16 NIV)

There comes a time when we will have to make our move, but we should not move in haste. We move instead with the footsteps of God, who has provided a way forward for us to travel. Once again, we are reminded to pay attention to God's voice and presence and not try to move or make a decision in haste.

The biggest question today is this: Do we trust in how and where God is leading?

Elijah had to trust that God was leading him in the right direction. He was running out of food and supplies. He knew he had to move on. He followed where God would lead. That's when Elijah came across the widow.

Elijah had no supplies and probably was tired from his journey. He was looking for someone to help him along the way, someone who could provide food and a place to rest. Instead, he likely saw the meager estate where the widow and her son lived, but this didn't stop Elijah from asking for help.

Some people are willing to help, even if it costs them a lot. The Lord honored the compassion of the widow and granted there would be enough food for her and her son. This is an Old Testament parallel to the Feeding of the Five Thousand in the New Testament, and it also reminds us to be in a place of trust.

God knows what he is doing. It takes guts to step out in faith and move to new areas—a new location or a new position. This requires courage and trust that God is with us, but we don't need to worry because God is with us.

The question is, do you hear his voice leading you? When you hear his voice, take the step of faith. Then, find ways to serve and trust God's timing in all things. Throughout scripture, there are periods of rest, and serving brings us closer to the answer.

Maybe you think you already know to what God is leading you, or perhaps you haven't stepped out in faith to serve. Who will you find on the path to serve? Those people might be part of God's plan for your next move.

Let's pray: Lord Jesus, guide me, and reveal yourself and your direction to me.

WESLEY COVENANT PRAYER

I am no longer my own, but yours.
Put me to what you will,
rank me with whom you will;
put me to doing,
put me to suffering;
let me be employed for you,
or laid aside for you,
exalted for you,
or brought low for you;
let me be full, let me be empty,
let me have all things,
let me have nothing:
I freely and wholeheartedly yield all things
to your pleasure and disposal.
And now, glorious and blessed God,
Father, Son and Holy Spirit,
you are mine and I am yours.
So be it.
And the covenant now made on earth,
let it be ratified in heaven.
Amen.

DAILY REFLECTION

Write about how you experienced God today and what God said to you. How is it with your soul regarding the choice(s) ahead of you?

Some time later the son of the woman who owned the house became ill. He grew worse and worse, and finally stopped breathing. She said to Elijah, "What do you have against me, man of God? Did you come to remind me of my sin and kill my son?" "Give me your son," Elijah replied. He took him from her arms, carried him to the upper room where he was staying, and laid him on his bed. Then he cried out to the Lord, "Lord my God, have you brought tragedy even on this widow I am staying with, by causing her son to die?" Then he stretched himself out on the boy three times and cried out to the Lord, "Lord my God, let this boy's life return to him!" The Lord heard Elijah's cry, and the boy's life returned to him, and he lived. Elijah picked up the child and carried him down from the room into the house. He gave him to his mother and said, "Look, your son is alive!" Then the woman said to Elijah, "Now I know that you are a man of God and that the word of the Lord from your mouth is the truth." (1 Kings 17:17–24 NIV)

You already may know the kind of life to which you have been called, but are you ready to handle whatever will come your way? Do you know the heartache you'll experience around you and that the presence of God is with you?

Keep your focus on the power of God, trusting his Word will not come back empty. Believe, and keep your faith in the truth that God is still working and desiring to make himself known.

How resilient are you in challenges? Are you ready to experience and bring the power of God to a hurting world in a different way than you have before? God has sent you and asks you to trust him when it seems hopeless.

Plead with God for his reign and power. Call upon him to make himself known in and through your life. Through the gift of faith, trust that God will be glorified and reveal himself through you in the path you decide to live out your faith and calling or purpose.

To where or to what do you sense God leading you? Do you have a confident answer yet? Can you see how God will reveal himself through you? Be sure to look for his power at work.

Look for the hand of the Lord.

Let's pray: Lord Jesus, guide me, and reveal yourself and your direction to me.

WESLEY COVENANT PRAYER

I am no longer my own, but yours.
Put me to what you will,
rank me with whom you will;
put me to doing,
put me to suffering;
let me be employed for you,
or laid aside for you,
exalted for you,
or brought low for you;
let me be full, let me be empty,
let me have all things,
let me have nothing:
I freely and wholeheartedly yield all things
to your pleasure and disposal.
And now, glorious and blessed God,
Father, Son and Holy Spirit,
you are mine and I am yours.

So be it.
And the covenant now made on earth,
let it be ratified in heaven.
Amen.

DAILY REFLECTION

Write about how you experienced God today and what God said to you. How is it with your soul regarding the choice(s) ahead of you?

Today is a day of Sabbath rest. Use this day to connect with and praise God, and reflect on how you have experienced God in this past week.

Read: Psalm 145

Reflect: How have you experienced God's grace this past week? Who do you believe God is transforming you to become?

Let's pray: Lord Jesus, guide me, and reveal yourself and your direction to me.

WESLEY COVENANT PRAYER

I am no longer my own, but yours.
Put me to what you will,
rank me with whom you will;
put me to doing,
put me to suffering;
let me be employed for you,
or laid aside for you,
exalted for you,
or brought low for you;
let me be full, let me be empty,
let me have all things,
let me have nothing:
I freely and wholeheartedly yield all things
to your pleasure and disposal.
And now, glorious and blessed God,

Father, Son and Holy Spirit,
you are mine and I am yours.
So be it.
And the covenant now made on earth,
let it be ratified in heaven.
Amen.

After a long time, in the third year, the word of the Lord came to Elijah: "Go and present yourself to Ahab, and I will send rain on the land." So Elijah went to present himself to Ahab. Now the famine was severe in Samaria, and Ahab had summoned Obadiah, his palace administrator. (Obadiah was a devout believer in the Lord. While Jezebel was killing off the Lord's prophets, Obadiah had taken a hundred prophets and hidden them in two caves, fifty in each, and had supplied them with food and water.) Ahab had said to Obadiah, "Go through the land to all the springs and valleys. Maybe we can find some grass to keep the horses and mules alive so we will not have to kill any of our animals." So they divided the land they were to cover, Ahab going in one direction and Obadiah in another. As Obadiah was walking along, Elijah met him. Obadiah recognized him, bowed down to the ground, and said, "Is it really you, my Lord Elijah?" "Yes," he replied. "Go tell your master, 'Elijah is here.'" "What have I done wrong," asked Obadiah, "that you are handing your servant over to Ahab to be put to death? As surely as the Lord your God lives, there is not a nation or kingdom where my master has not sent someone to look for you. And whenever a nation or kingdom claimed you were not there, he made them swear they could not find you. But now you tell me to go to my master and say, 'Elijah is here.' I don't know where the Spirit of the Lord may carry you when I leave you. If I go and tell Ahab and he doesn't find you, he will kill me. Yet I your servant have worshiped the Lord since my youth. Haven't you heard, my Lord, what I did while Jezebel was killing the prophets of the Lord? I hid a hundred of the Lord's prophets in two caves, fifty in each, and supplied them with food and water. And now you tell me to go to my master and say, 'Elijah is here.' He will kill me!" Elijah said, "As the Lord Almighty lives, whom I serve, I will surely present myself to Ahab today." (1 Kings 18:1–15 NIV)

God has called you. God has equipped you to do his mission. Unfortunately, some people will not understand. People will try to tear you down. Do you have resolve to stay the course? How will you handle opposition that comes your way?

Elijah knew, most likely, how his presence would be handled. He knew what was going on. Yet Obadiah tried to get Elijah to change course. Are people trying to convince you to take a "safe" route? Are people trying to protect you? There could be godly wisdom in what someone tells you.

It's awesome to have these people because they're looking out for you in the way they know how. Still, you must discern their motives. Are they keeping you from fully living into your calling? Or could they be warning you of impending dangers? Listen carefully. Could it be the enemy speaking through them (like the apostle Peter in Matthew 16)? Or is God trying to help you understand what is likely to happen?

Be sure to pay attention because this is part of the discerning process. These are things to think about *and* talk about with God.

Know this: God has called you. Follow his lead. Listen carefully. Let nothing stop your calling or hinder your walk with God.

Just be sure you are going with God and not your pride.

Let's pray: Lord Jesus, guide me, and reveal yourself and your direction to me.

WESLEY COVENANT PRAYER

I am no longer my own, but yours.
Put me to what you will,
rank me with whom you will;
put me to doing,
put me to suffering;
let me be employed for you,
or laid aside for you,
exalted for you,
or brought low for you;
let me be full, let me be empty,
let me have all things,
let me have nothing:
I freely and wholeheartedly yield all things
to your pleasure and disposal.
And now, glorious and blessed God,
Father, Son and Holy Spirit,
you are mine and I am yours.
So be it.
And the covenant now made on earth,
let it be ratified in heaven.
Amen.

DAILY REFLECTION

Write about how you experienced God today and what God said to you. How is it with your soul regarding the choice(s) ahead of you?

So Obadiah went to meet Ahab and told him, and Ahab went to meet Elijah. When he saw Elijah, he said to him, "Is that you, you troubler of Israel?" "I have not made trouble for Israel," Elijah replied. "But you and your father's family have. You have abandoned the Lord's commands and have followed the Baals. Now summon the people from all over Israel to meet me on Mount Carmel. And bring the four hundred and fifty prophets of Baal and the four hundred prophets of Asherah, who eat at Jezebel's table." So Ahab sent word throughout all Israel and assembled the prophets on Mount Carmel. Elijah went before the people and said, "How long will you waver between two opinions? If the Lord is God, follow him; but if Baal is God, follow him." But the people said nothing.
(1 Kings 18:16–21 NIV)

Knowing what you stand for is vital. Keeping your convictions is crucial. Yes, there will be opposition along the way, but the truth of God is more powerful.

Be prepared for the opposition to come from inside you and from outside sources.

What are some your non-negotiables that reveal your convictions about life? About what is right and wrong? About what you know of yourself? What are the boundaries you will not cross? You must know this, or you will get run over by others.

As you take this time to discern the next steps, trust that your convictions will challenge you. Then, people will ask you to compromise, all for keeping the peace. But is this what God wants you to do?

Gut-check time: how will you stand up for truth, especially when the truth may go against the culture?

Let's pray: Lord Jesus, guide me, and reveal yourself and your direction to me.

WESLEY COVENANT PRAYER

I am no longer my own, but yours.
Put me to what you will,
rank me with whom you will;
put me to doing,
put me to suffering;
let me be employed for you,
or laid aside for you,
exalted for you,
or brought low for you;
let me be full, let me be empty,
let me have all things,
let me have nothing:
I freely and wholeheartedly yield all things
to your pleasure and disposal.
And now, glorious and blessed God,
Father, Son and Holy Spirit,
you are mine and I am yours.
So be it.
And the covenant now made on earth,
let it be ratified in heaven.
Amen.

DAILY REFLECTION

Write about how you experienced God today and what God said to you. How is it with your soul regarding the choice(s) ahead of you?

Then Elijah said to them, "I am the only one of the Lord's prophets left, but Baal has four hundred and fifty prophets. Get two bulls for us. Let Baal's prophets choose one for themselves, and let them cut it into pieces and put it on the wood but not set fire to it. I will prepare the other bull and put it on the wood but not set fire to it. Then you call on the name of your god, and I will call on the name of the Lord. The god who answers by fire—he is God." Then all the people said, "What you say is good." (1 Kings 18:22–24 NIV)

Desperation or confidence? This is a decision that takes time and direction. We also have to ask if we are making this decision out of our faith in Christ or if we are desperate to hold on and not make the "wrong" decision.

Elijah felt that he was all alone. He seems to have forgotten Obadiah had said one hundred prophets were hidden away for safety. Out of desperation, Elijah made a big and bold stand. It was almost like he was testing God, but he also showed how the people were worshipping a false god. They had their hope in something futile and frail.

Where is your hope today? Are you desperate because you feel alone? Is your confidence, trust, and faith in the one true God or something disposable?

When deciding, pay attention to what you're giving time and attention. Cling and trust in the God who is guiding you. Look to his cross for your confidence. Witness the empty tomb for your hope.

Let's pray: Lord Jesus, guide me, and reveal yourself and your direction to me.

WESLEY COVENANT PRAYER

I am no longer my own, but yours.
Put me to what you will,
rank me with whom you will;
put me to doing,
put me to suffering;
let me be employed for you,
or laid aside for you,
exalted for you,
or brought low for you;
let me be full, let me be empty,
let me have all things,
let me have nothing:
I freely and wholeheartedly yield all things
to your pleasure and disposal.
And now, glorious and blessed God,
Father, Son and Holy Spirit,
you are mine and I am yours.
So be it.
And the covenant now made on earth,
let it be ratified in heaven.
Amen.

DAILY REFLECTION

Write about how you experienced God today and what God said to you. How is it with your soul regarding the choice(s) ahead of you?

DAY 11

Elijah said to the prophets of Baal, "Choose one of the bulls and prepare it first, since there are so many of you. Call on the name of your god, but do not light the fire." So they took the bull given them and prepared it. Then they called on the name of Baal from morning till noon. "Baal, answer us!" they shouted. But there was no response; no one answered. And they danced around the altar they had made. At noon Elijah began to taunt them. "Shout louder!" he said. "Surely he is a god! Perhaps he is deep in thought, or busy, or traveling. Maybe he is sleeping and must be awakened." So they shouted louder and slashed themselves with swords and spears, as was their custom, until their blood flowed. Midday passed, and they continued their frantic prophesying until the time for the evening sacrifice. But there was no response, no one answered, no one paid attention. (1 Kings 18:25–29 NIV)

Our false gods will hold us captive, making us think we can count on them because they'll be there. False gods refer to anything other than the Lord that we place in high esteem to make us feel better or to give us something to worship and work for.

What are you counting on for the future? Will your life be complete and fulfilled by whatever you're counting on? What will happen to you when other foundations fall out from under you?

Today is another gut-check day. Today, you will find out if you look foolish. Pay attention to who or what you are counting on for help. Only the true God will answer. Listen for his voice. God is never too preoccupied to listen or to respond to you.

Once again, is your confidence for the future solely in God? Or are you counting on anything else?

Let's pray: Lord Jesus, guide me, and reveal yourself and your direction to me.

WESLEY COVENANT PRAYER

I am no longer my own, but yours.
Put me to what you will,
rank me with whom you will;
put me to doing,
put me to suffering;
let me be employed for you,
or laid aside for you,
exalted for you,
or brought low for you;
let me be full, let me be empty,
let me have all things,
let me have nothing:
I freely and wholeheartedly yield all things
to your pleasure and disposal.
And now, glorious and blessed God,
Father, Son and Holy Spirit,
you are mine and I am yours.
So be it.
And the covenant now made on earth,
let it be ratified in heaven.
Amen.

DAILY REFLECTION

Write about how you experienced God today and what God said to you. How is it with your soul regarding the choice(s) ahead of you?

Then Elijah said to all the people, "Come here to me." They came to him, and he repaired the altar of the Lord, which had been torn down. Elijah took twelve stones, one for each of the tribes descended from Jacob, to whom the word of the Lord had come, saying, "Your name shall be Israel." With the stones he built an altar in the name of the Lord, and he dug a trench around it large enough to hold two seahs of seed. He arranged the wood, cut the bull into pieces and laid it on the wood. Then he said to them, "Fill four large jars with water and pour it on the offering and on the wood." "Do it again," he said, and they did it again. "Do it a third time," he ordered, and they did it the third time. The water ran down around the altar and even filled the trench. At the time of sacrifice, the prophet Elijah stepped forward and prayed: "Lord, the God of Abraham, Isaac and Israel, let it be known today that you are God in Israel and that I am your servant and have done all these things at your command. Answer me, Lord, answer me, so these people will know that you, Lord, are God, and that you are turning their hearts back again." Then the fire of the Lord fell and burned up the sacrifice, the wood, the stones and the soil, and also licked up the water in the trench. When all the people saw this, they fell prostrate and cried, "The Lord—he is God! The Lord—he is God!" (1 Kings 18:30–39 NIV)

Today is another day we take time to evaluate our priorities. We've done this a lot lately, but it's vital that we do so daily.

Notice how Elijah has to rebuild the altar. Is there any part of your relationship with God that needs to be repaired or rebuilt? This is the focus for today—have you done this already? Ask God to which altars or idols you bow down. Ask God where you trust something or someone else more than him.

Again, is your confidence in God alone, or are you counting on anyone or anything else to bail you out?

Elijah took a stand to demonstrate God's awesome power and presence so the rest of the people could see God's presence and follow him—and him alone.

Look for how God asks you to respond to taunts and jeers from the crowd. You are the image and representative of God. You are a royal priest. This is your calling.

Your decision may seem challenging, but the best decision always stands for truth and shows how God is present and working among his people.

Stand firm in God's truth, and you will see the direction in which you should go. Are you ready to stand for something, even if people go in a different direction? You need to answer that question for yourself.

Let's pray: Lord Jesus, guide me, and reveal yourself and your direction to me.

WESLEY COVENANT PRAYER

I am no longer my own, but yours.
Put me to what you will,
rank me with whom you will;
put me to doing,
put me to suffering;
let me be employed for you,
or laid aside for you,

exalted for you,
or brought low for you;
let me be full, let me be empty,
let me have all things,
let me have nothing:
I freely and wholeheartedly yield all things
to your pleasure and disposal.
And now, glorious and blessed God,
Father, Son and Holy Spirit,
you are mine and I am yours.
So be it.
And the covenant now made on earth,
let it be ratified in heaven.
Amen.

DAILY REFLECTION

Write about how you experienced God today and what God said to you. How is it with your soul regarding the choice(s) ahead of you?

Then Elijah commanded them, "Seize the prophets of Baal. Don't let anyone get away!" They seized them, and Elijah had them brought down to the Kishon Valley and slaughtered there. And Elijah said to Ahab, "Go, eat and drink, for there is the sound of a heavy rain." So Ahab went off to eat and drink, but Elijah climbed to the top of Carmel, bent down to the ground and put his face between his knees. "Go and look toward the sea," he told his servant. And he went up and looked. "There is nothing there," he said. Seven times Elijah said, "Go back." The seventh time the servant reported, "A cloud as small as a man's hand is rising from the sea." So Elijah said, "Go and tell Ahab, 'Hitch up your chariot and go down before the rain stops you.'" Meanwhile, the sky grew black with clouds, the wind rose, a heavy rain started falling and Ahab rode off to Jezreel. The power of the Lord came on Elijah and, tucking his cloak into his belt, he ran ahead of Ahab all the way to Jezreel. (1 Kings 18:40–46 NIV)

This may seem like a strange passage for today's discernment process, but look closely.

When you think you have made a decision, you must ensure it aligns with what the Lord is speaking and doing. You may have had complete confidence in your decision, but today, take some time and pay attention.

Today may be a day when you're seeking a sign or a response

that indicates you've made the right choice. Today is most likely when taking a break and fasting is required. Remember that Jesus spent forty full days being filled with the Holy Spirit before he was tempted. This time is essential for you.

I can quickly jump the gun and make a rash decision. Maybe you can, too, so look at the passage again.

Seven times. Seven times Elijah's servant went to check to see if there were clouds. It would be easy to give up after the first time that we went out and saw nothing. But God's timing is not our timing. It is vital to keep returning to the Lord, resting and trusting in him, before we move forward. We may decide on the right choice, but do we have the skills for our next moves? Are we the persons we need to be when making our next moves?

Today we fast. We need to take a break from what distracts us, and use that time to call out to God. We need to give up something physically (like food) to make room to hear from heaven, spiritually. We may or may not receive affirmation of our decisions.

For several days, we have been paying attention to who God is. This is the day to focus on who God desires us to be. Keep stepping out and looking on the horizon to see what God is doing. We do this to stay grounded in God. When we're grounded in God, we will not go to our comforts to satisfy ourselves; we will do something different from everyone else. We will put ourselves in positions to experience the one true God.

Find a time today to fast. Then, be persistent in calling out to God.

Suggested Read: John Wesley's sermon "The Circumcision of the Heart"

You can read the full sermon at http://wesley.nnu.edu/john-wesley/the-sermons-of-john-wesley-1872-edition/sermon-17-the-circumcision-of-the-heart.

Let's pray: Lord Jesus, guide me, and reveal yourself and your direction to me.

WESLEY COVENANT PRAYER

I am no longer my own, but yours.
Put me to what you will,
rank me with whom you will;
put me to doing,
put me to suffering;
let me be employed for you,
or laid aside for you,
exalted for you,
or brought low for you;
let me be full, let me be empty,
let me have all things,
let me have nothing:
I freely and wholeheartedly yield all things
to your pleasure and disposal.
And now, glorious and blessed God,
Father, Son and Holy Spirit,
you are mine and I am yours.
So be it.
And the covenant now made on earth,
let it be ratified in heaven.
Amen.

DAILY REFLECTION

Write about how you experienced God today and what God said to you. How is it with your soul regarding the choice(s) ahead of you?

DAY 14 REFLECTION

Today is a day of Sabbath rest. Use this day to connect with and praise God, and reflect on how you have experienced God in this past week.

Read: Psalm 146

Reflect: How have you experienced God's grace this past week? Who do you believe God is calling you to serve?

Let's pray: Lord Jesus, guide me, and reveal yourself and your direction to me.

WESLEY COVENANT PRAYER

I am no longer my own, but yours.
Put me to what you will,
rank me with whom you will;
put me to doing,
put me to suffering;
let me be employed for you,
or laid aside for you,
exalted for you,
or brought low for you;
let me be full, let me be empty,
let me have all things,
let me have nothing:
I freely and wholeheartedly yield all things
to your pleasure and disposal.
And now, glorious and blessed God,

Father, Son and Holy Spirit,
you are mine and I am yours.
So be it.
And the covenant now made on earth,
let it be ratified in heaven.
Amen.

Now Ahab told Jezebel everything Elijah had done and how he had killed all the prophets with the sword. So Jezebel sent a messenger to Elijah to say, "May the gods deal with me, be it ever so severely, if by this time tomorrow I do not make your life like that of one of them." Elijah was afraid and ran for his life. When he came to Beersheba in Judah, he left his servant there, while he himself went a day's journey into the wilderness. He came to a broom bush, sat down under it and prayed that he might die. "I have had enough, Lord," he said. "Take my life; I am no better than my ancestors." Then he lay down under the bush and fell asleep. All at once an angel touched him and said, "Get up and eat." He looked around, and there by his head was some bread baked over hot coals, and a jar of water. He ate and drank and then lay down again. The angel of the Lord came back a second time and touched him and said, "Get up and eat, for the journey is too much for you." So he got up and ate and drank. Strengthened by that food, he traveled forty days and forty nights until he reached Horeb, the mountain of God. There he went into a cave and spent the night. And the word of the Lord came to him: "What are you doing here, Elijah?"
(1 Kings 19:1–9 NIV)

Today may be a good day to reflect on how the decision-making process is affecting you. How much pressure are you putting on yourself? On your organization? Remember that some people will be angry with you whichever way you choose because they may not fully understand how God is working in you, but you can be assured that God is with you and is guiding you.

In the passage, we meet Elijah on the run. He's made some bold moves, and now the leadership of Israel is trying to get rid of him. Elijah's pressure is too much, so he pleads with the Lord to end it all. He doesn't see the value in continuing. It is too difficult. But this does not stop God.

God is constantly finding ways to provide comfort and rest for his people, which is why we need to pause and reflect today. God knows how challenging and overwhelming life and decisions are in our lives. Does God say we need to stop and forget it?

Nope.

God, instead, will find a way to provide some relief for the moment. Then, when we can stop and rest, we will allow God to fill us with his joy for our lives and work once again. We need to take a break and try not to think about the decisions we need to make. There is still time.

Rest. Nap. Chill out. Whatever you need to do, ask God to give you what you need to continue the journey so you can be faithful to God.

What will you do today?

Challenge: Take at least an hour and do something out of the ordinary to take your mind off from the decision process. Praise God. Listen to some music. Pray. Sit in silence. Mow the lawn. Do whatever will help you rest in the presence of God.

Let's pray: Lord Jesus, guide me, and reveal yourself and your direction to me.

WESLEY COVENANT PRAYER

I am no longer my own, but yours.
Put me to what you will,
rank me with whom you will;
put me to doing,
put me to suffering;
let me be employed for you,
or laid aside for you,
exalted for you,
or brought low for you;
let me be full, let me be empty,
let me have all things,
let me have nothing:
I freely and wholeheartedly yield all things
to your pleasure and disposal.
And now, glorious and blessed God,
Father, Son and Holy Spirit,
you are mine and I am yours.
So be it.
And the covenant now made on earth,
let it be ratified in heaven.
Amen.

DAILY REFLECTION

Write about how you experienced God today and what God said to you. How is it with your soul regarding the choice(s) ahead of you?

There he went into a cave and spent the night. And the word of the Lord came to him: "What are you doing here, Elijah?" He replied, "I have been very zealous for the Lord God Almighty. The Israelites have rejected your covenant, torn down your altars, and put your prophets to death with the sword. I am the only one left, and now they are trying to kill me too." The Lord said, "Go out and stand on the mountain in the presence of the Lord, for the Lord is about to pass by." Then a great and powerful wind tore the mountains apart and shattered the rocks before the Lord, but the Lord was not in the wind. After the wind there was an earthquake, but the Lord was not in the earthquake. After the earthquake came a fire, but the Lord was not in the fire. And after the fire came a gentle whisper. When Elijah heard it, he pulled his cloak over his face and went out and stood at the mouth of the cave. Then a voice said to him, "What are you doing here, Elijah?" He replied, "I have been very zealous for the Lord God Almighty. The Israelites have rejected your covenant, torn down your altars, and put your prophets to death with the sword. I am the only one left, and now they are trying to kill me too." The Lord said to him, "Go back the way you came, and go to the Desert of Damascus. When you get there, anoint Hazael king over Aram." (1 Kings 19:9–15 NIV)

We have spent time alone, listening to God. We also sought the presence of God and paid attention to where the voices to which we're listening are coming from—God or somewhere or someone else.

Who are you trying to please?

No one ever said that life is easy. We all need breaks from time to time. We may feel like we're running on empty, but we can never run away from God. He is always with us.

You may be like Elijah, trying to run away and hide, and hear God asking, "What are you doing here?" In other words, why are you in this position? What got you to the place you are in right now? This isn't because God doesn't know the answer. You are asked these questions to show you what you have done and experienced to get to where you are now.

God knows. Maybe he just wants you to be in a place to see his hand guiding you, rather than blaming others for your situation.

After you express yourself to God, God might redirect you. He may not give you any reasons, but he may remind you to keep going. Keep going with what you know to do. It is possible you'll find answers in working and continuing to serve.

Let's pray: Lord Jesus, guide me, and reveal yourself and your direction to me.

WESLEY COVENANT PRAYER

I am no longer my own, but yours.
Put me to what you will,
rank me with whom you will;
put me to doing,
put me to suffering;
let me be employed for you,
or laid aside for you,
exalted for you,
or brought low for you;

let me be full, let me be empty,
let me have all things,
let me have nothing:
I freely and wholeheartedly yield all things
to your pleasure and disposal.
And now, glorious and blessed God,
Father, Son and Holy Spirit,
you are mine and I am yours.
So be it.
And the covenant now made on earth,
let it be ratified in heaven.
Amen.

DAILY REFLECTION

Write about how you experienced God today and what God said to
you. How is it with your soul regarding the choice(s) ahead of you?

"Also, anoint Jehu son of Nimshi king over Israel, and anoint Elisha son of Shaphat from Abel Meholah to succeed you as prophet. Jehu will put to death any who escape the sword of Hazael, and Elisha will put to death any who escape the sword of Jehu. Yet I reserve seven thousand in Israel—all whose knees have not bowed down to Baal and whose mouths have not kissed him." So Elijah went from there and found Elisha son of Shaphat. He was plowing with twelve yoke of oxen, and he himself was driving the twelfth pair. Elijah went up to him and threw his cloak around him. Elisha then left his oxen and ran after Elijah. "Let me kiss my father and mother goodbye," he said, "and then I will come with you." "Go back," Elijah replied. "What have I done to you?" So Elisha left him and went back. He took his yoke of oxen and slaughtered them. He burned the plowing equipment to cook the meat and gave it to the people, and they ate. Then he set out to follow Elijah and became his servant. (1 Kings 19:16–21 NIV)

We have been concentrating on two big focal points:

1. Looking at and understanding who God is which leads us to understand who we were meant to be
2. Stepping out in faith to keep doing what God has already called us to do

Today is a good day to pause all decisions—try this. Then, ask yourself if you're the only one involved in the decision process.

It is easy to feel alone and as if everything hangs on what you do. The truth is, you don't need to make decisions independently. If you're paying attention, you'll see that God always brings us people to help carry the burdens.

Again, pause today. See who God may have put in your path to do this with you. Look at how many others God has kept safe to live out their callings.

You can trust God to make sure you are never alone.

Let's pray: Lord Jesus, guide me, and reveal yourself and your direction to me.

WESLEY COVENANT PRAYER

I am no longer my own, but yours.
Put me to what you will,
rank me with whom you will;
put me to doing,
put me to suffering;
let me be employed for you,
or laid aside for you,
exalted for you,
or brought low for you;
let me be full, let me be empty,
let me have all things,
let me have nothing:
I freely and wholeheartedly yield all things
to your pleasure and disposal.
And now, glorious and blessed God,
Father, Son and Holy Spirit,
you are mine and I am yours.
So be it.

And the covenant now made on earth,
let it be ratified in heaven.
Amen.

DAILY REFLECTION

Write about how you experienced God today and what God said to you. How is it with your soul regarding the choice(s) ahead of you?

Now Ben-Hadad king of Aram mustered his entire army. Accompanied by thirty-two kings with their horses and chariots, he went up and besieged Samaria and attacked it. He sent messengers into the city to Ahab king of Israel, saying, "This is what Ben-Hadad says: 'Your silver and gold are mine, and the best of your wives and children are mine.'" The king of Israel answered, "Just as you say, my Lord the king. I and all I have are yours." The messengers came again and said, "This is what Ben-Hadad says: 'I sent to demand your silver and gold, your wives and your children. But about this time tomorrow I am going to send my officials to search your palace and the houses of your officials. They will seize everything you value and carry it away.'" The king of Israel summoned all the elders of the land and said to them, "See how this man is looking for trouble! When he sent for my wives and my children, my silver and my gold, I did not refuse him." The elders and the people all answered, "Don't listen to him or agree to his demands." So he replied to Ben-Hadad's messengers, "Tell my Lord the king, 'Your servant will do all you demanded the first time, but this demand I cannot meet.'" They left and took the answer back to Ben-Hadad. Then Ben-Hadad sent another message to Ahab: "May the gods deal with me, be it ever so severely, if enough dust remains in Samaria to give each of my men a handful." The king of Israel answered,

"Tell him: 'One who puts on his armor should not boast like one who takes it off.'" Ben-Hadad heard this message while he and the kings were drinking in their tents, and he ordered his men: "Prepare to attack." So they prepared to attack the city." (1 Kings 20:1–12 NIV)

You have been given a lot. You have been given all you need. You have been given all God's blessings under heaven (Ephesians 1). Does this make you arrogant or too confident in your talents?

The other side is this: what are you willing to give up? This does not mean you should compromise what you've been given. Enemies will make demands on you to do what they want. It'll come under the guise of trying to help you preserve your way of life, but don't give in to the enemy.

The path God has you on is not for the faint of heart. It is not for just anyone. God has you here, in this position, because he knows what he's doing. He knows what he's created you for.

You may be in a situation like Ben Hadad or King Ahab, and you are in a position to show who you trust more—your stuff and your talents or the one true God who is guiding and leading you.

You will always have enemies and those who want to attack, but you also have God on your side.

Today, Read Romans 8 and reflect on that chapter to see what the Holy Spirit speaks to you.

Let's pray: Lord Jesus, guide me, and reveal yourself and your direction to me.

WESLEY COVENANT PRAYER

I am no longer my own, but yours.
Put me to what you will,
rank me with whom you will;
put me to doing,

put me to suffering;
let me be employed for you,
or laid aside for you,
exalted for you,
or brought low for you;
let me be full, let me be empty,
let me have all things,
let me have nothing:
I freely and wholeheartedly yield all things
to your pleasure and disposal.
And now, glorious and blessed God,
Father, Son and Holy Spirit,
you are mine and I am yours.
So be it.
And the covenant now made on earth,
let it be ratified in heaven.
Amen.

DAILY REFLECTION

Write about how you experienced God today and what God said to you. How is it with your soul regarding the choice(s) ahead of you?

Meanwhile a prophet came to Ahab king of Israel and announced, "This is what the Lord says: 'Do you see this vast army? I will give it into your hand today, and then you will know that I am the Lord.'" "But who will do this?" asked Ahab. The prophet replied, "This is what the Lord says: 'The junior officers under the provincial commanders will do it.'" "And who will start the battle?" he asked. The prophet answered, "You will." So Ahab summoned the 232 junior officers under the provincial commanders. Then he assembled the rest of the Israelites, 7,000 in all. They set out at noon while Ben-Hadad and the 32 kings allied with him were in their tents getting drunk. The junior officers under the provincial commanders went out first. Now Ben-Hadad had dispatched scouts, who reported, "Men are advancing from Samaria." He said, "If they have come out for peace, take them alive; if they have come out for war, take them alive." The junior officers under the provincial commanders marched out of the city with the army behind them and each one struck down his opponent. At that, the Arameans fled, with the Israelites in pursuit. But Ben-Hadad king of Aram escaped on horseback with some of his horsemen. The king of Israel advanced and overpowered the horses and chariots and inflicted heavy losses on the Arameans. Afterward, the prophet came to the king of Israel and said, "Strengthen your position and see what must be done, because next spring the king of Aram will attack you again." (1 Kings 20:13–22 NIV)

This may seem like a strange passage in the discernment process. We're not off to defeat another army, right? But what if we are? What if there is a spiritual army out to get you? In other words, do you know what or who your enemy is?

We all have enemies who try to stop us, but most of the time, these enemies are within us. Anxiety. Fear. Worry. Stress. Insecurity. You name it. You may also have other enemies holding you back. You'll never decide with these enemies controlling you.

Today is a day of fasting.

True, we don't know what the future will hold, but we do know *who* holds the future. Will we take this time to fast and allow God to show us how to defeat the enemies that stop us?

Will you take this time to see how God works in and through you so that you can have the future he's designed for you?

Challenge: Your decision and success depends on your trust in God and in allowing God to win the battle over your mind. As you fast today, focus on these two passages (at least):

- 2 Corinthians 10:1–5
- Philippians 4:4–9

Let's pray: Lord Jesus, guide me, and reveal yourself and your direction to me.

WESLEY COVENANT PRAYER

I am no longer my own, but yours.
Put me to what you will,
rank me with whom you will;
put me to doing,
put me to suffering;

let me be employed for you,
or laid aside for you,
exalted for you,
or brought low for you;
let me be full, let me be empty,
let me have all things,
let me have nothing:
I freely and wholeheartedly yield all things
to your pleasure and disposal.
And now, glorious and blessed God,
Father, Son and Holy Spirit,
you are mine and I am yours.
So be it.
And the covenant now made on earth,
let it be ratified in heaven.
Amen.

DAILY REFLECTION

Write about how you experienced God today and what God said to you. How is it with your soul regarding the choice(s) ahead of you?

Meanwhile, the officials of the king of Aram advised him, "Their gods are gods of the hills. That is why they were too strong for us. But if we fight them on the plains, surely we will be stronger than they. Do this: Remove all the kings from their commands and replace them with other officers. You must also raise an army like the one you lost—horse for horse and chariot for chariot—so we can fight Israel on the plains. Then surely we will be stronger than they." He agreed with them and acted accordingly. The next spring Ben-Hadad mustered the Arameans and went up to Aphek to fight against Israel. When the Israelites were also mustered and given provisions, they marched out to meet them. The Israelites camped opposite them like two small flocks of goats, while the Arameans covered the countryside. The man of God came up and told the king of Israel, "This is what the Lord says: 'Because the Arameans think the Lord is a god of the hills and not a god of the valleys, I will deliver this vast army into your hands, and you will know that I am the Lord.'" For seven days they camped opposite each other, and on the seventh day the battle was joined. The Israelites inflicted a hundred thousand casualties on the Aramean foot soldiers in one day. The rest of them escaped to the city of Aphek, where the wall collapsed on twenty-seven thousand of them. And Ben-Hadad fled to the city and hid in an inner room. His officials said to him, "Look, we have heard that the kings of Israel are merciful. Let us go to the king of Israel with sackcloth around our waists and ropes around our heads. Perhaps he will spare your life." Wearing sackcloth around their waists and ropes around their heads, they went to the king of Israel and said, "Your servant Ben-Hadad says: 'Please let me live.'" The king answered, "Is he still alive? He is my brother." The men took this as a good sign and were quick to pick up his word. "Yes, your brother Ben-Hadad!" they said. "Go and get him," the king said. When Ben-Hadad came out, Ahab had him come up into his chariot. "I will return the cities my father took from your father," Ben-Hadad offered. "You may set up your own market areas in Damascus, as my father did in Samaria." Ahab said, "On the basis of a treaty I will set you free." So he made a treaty with him, and let him go. (1 Kings 20:23–34 NIV)

Here is one of the beautiful aspects of scripture. Even if the situation in the narrative is not exactly what you're going through, the Holy Spirit will still speak the truth to apply to your situation. Today's passage is a perfect example of this.

You need to ask yourself, "How is my reputation?" In other words, for what are you known? This question will help with the discernment process. You have to understand what you are known for.

Why? Because you need to consider if people will be able to work with you, depending on your reputation. Are you generous? Are you easily angered? Modest? Arrogant? Stingy? Lazy? Take some time to think about your good qualities.

Remember, we're learning more about God's presence and who God is, but at the same time, we are learning more about ourselves to see where and how God is moving and working within and through us. We're learning to see the good God has placed within us.

Reread the passage for today. The enemy asked for mercy. How far are you willing to go to help people experience the grace of God you have experienced? This doesn't mean you must put yourself in a harmful situation or allow yourself to be manipulated or run over. But you do need to know your boundaries.

As you are making this decision, I pray you are also learning where your boundaries are so you can live the life to which you have been called. What would you consider "crossing the line" so that you wouldn't consider extending grace? Knowing this will help you see where God is still shaping your heart and thinking. This also will reveal opportunities for your past actions and hurts to be healed by the presence of Jesus Christ so that you can move forward healthily.

Let's pray: Lord Jesus, guide me, and reveal yourself and your direction to me.

WESLEY COVENANT PRAYER

I am no longer my own, but yours.
Put me to what you will,
rank me with whom you will;
put me to doing,
put me to suffering;
let me be employed for you,
or laid aside for you,
exalted for you,
or brought low for you;
let me be full, let me be empty,
let me have all things,
let me have nothing:
I freely and wholeheartedly yield all things
to your pleasure and disposal.
And now, glorious and blessed God,

Father, Son and Holy Spirit,
you are mine and I am yours.
So be it.
And the covenant now made on earth,
let it be ratified in heaven.
Amen.

DAILY REFLECTION

Write about how you experienced God today and what God said to you. How is it with your soul regarding the choice(s) ahead of you?

Today is a day of Sabbath rest. Use this day to connect with and praise God, and reflect on how you have experienced God in this past week.

Read: Psalm 40

Reflect: How have you experienced God's grace in this past week? Where do you stand in this discernment process? Have you made up your mind, or are you still seeking God's wisdom and guidance?

Let's pray: Lord Jesus, guide me, and reveal yourself and your direction to me.

WESLEY COVENANT PRAYER

I am no longer my own, but yours.
Put me to what you will,
rank me with whom you will;
put me to doing,
put me to suffering;
let me be employed for you,
or laid aside for you,
exalted for you,
or brought low for you;
let me be full, let me be empty,
let me have all things,
let me have nothing:
I freely and wholeheartedly yield all things
to your pleasure and disposal.
And now, glorious and blessed God,
Father, Son and Holy Spirit,

you are mine and I am yours.
So be it.
And the covenant now made on earth,
let it be ratified in heaven.
Amen.

By the word of the Lord one of the company of the prophets said to his companion, "Strike me with your weapon," but he refused. So the prophet said, "Because you have not obeyed the Lord, as soon as you leave me a lion will kill you." And after the man went away, a lion found him and killed him. The prophet found another man and said, "Strike me, please." So the man struck him and wounded him. Then the prophet went and stood by the road waiting for the king. He disguised himself with his headband down over his eyes. As the king passed by, the prophet called out to him, "Your servant went into the thick of the battle, and someone came to me with a captive and said, 'Guard this man. If he is missing, it will be your life for his life, or you must pay a talent of silver.' While your servant was busy here and there, the man disappeared." "That is your sentence," the king of Israel said. "You have pronounced it yourself." Then the prophet quickly removed the headband from his eyes, and the king of Israel recognized him as one of the prophets. He said to the king, "This is what the Lord says: 'You have set free a man I had determined should die. Therefore it is your life for his life, your people for his people.'" Sullen and angry, the king of Israel went to his palace in Samaria. (1 Kings 20:35–43 NIV)

We're reading this passage today because we should never skip over the passages we don't like or that we think don't apply to us. The Holy Spirit has a message for us throughout scripture, and today's passage is no different.

As we continue this process of discernment, we need to take time to evaluate our obedience to God and his will. In other words, we need to make sure we genuinely seeking God's will, not fame, fortune, an easier life, or anything that is selfish and focuses entirely on us.

I saw the following quote from someone named Monte Dugger:

> The next time you call Christ 'Lord,' think of what that entails by using the acronym: LORD—which pledges that we, as bondservants, are to Lay Our Rights Down.

As I read that quote, it struck me that this is part of what it means to deny ourselves, pick up our cross, and follow Jesus. We seek to live for him and him alone. We strive to do his will because we know that his will leads us to life eternal—real life. We seek to do the will of God and obey him because our lives glorify him. And when our lives glorify God, we experience life in ways we never would have if we had lived solely for ourselves.

Today, consider the decision you are in the process of making. Ask yourself, "Am I obedient to God if I choose to [name decision]?" This may be a way to eliminate other options.

Don't have anxiety or even impatience when you're seeking to discern the next steps. Instead, seek to live in God's will and obey him in all you do.

The key to knowing what to do is to understand your convictions and stand by them. This can help you see how God leads you to make this decision.

We are over halfway to the end of our forty-day process! Keep it up! Try not to rush. Remember to sit still and seek God above all.

Let's pray: Lord Jesus, guide me, and reveal yourself and your direction to me.

WESLEY COVENANT PRAYER

I am no longer my own, but yours.
Put me to what you will,
rank me with whom you will;
put me to doing,
put me to suffering;
let me be employed for you,
or laid aside for you,
exalted for you,
or brought low for you;
let me be full, let me be empty,
let me have all things,
let me have nothing:
I freely and wholeheartedly yield all things
to your pleasure and disposal.
And now, glorious and blessed God,
Father, Son and Holy Spirit,
you are mine and I am yours.
So be it.
And the covenant now made on earth,
let it be ratified in heaven.
Amen.

DAILY REFLECTION

Write about what God has revealed about himself. How is it with your soul, just sitting in the presence of God? What is going through your mind and heart about the decision or choice you need to make?

Some time later there was an incident involving a vineyard belonging to Naboth the Jezreelite. The vineyard was in Jezreel, close to the palace of Ahab king of Samaria. Ahab said to Naboth, "Let me have your vineyard to use for a vegetable garden, since it is close to my palace. In exchange I will give you a better vineyard or, if you prefer, I will pay you whatever it is worth." But Naboth replied, "The Lord forbid that I should give you the inheritance of my ancestors." So Ahab went home, sullen and angry because Naboth the Jezreelite had said, "I will not give you the inheritance of my ancestors." He lay on his bed sulking and refused to eat. His wife Jezebel came in and asked him, "Why are you so sullen? Why won't you eat?" He answered her, "Because I said to Naboth the Jezreelite, 'Sell me your vineyard; or if you prefer, I will give you another vineyard in its place.' But he said, 'I will not give you my vineyard.'" Jezebel his wife said, "Is this how you act as king over Israel? Get up and eat! Cheer up. I'll get you the vineyard of Naboth the Jezreelite." So she wrote letters in Ahab's name, placed his seal on them, and sent them to the elders and nobles who lived in Naboth's city with him. In those letters she wrote: "Proclaim a day of fasting and seat Naboth in a prominent place among the people. But seat two scoundrels opposite him and have them bring charges that he has cursed both God and the king. Then take him out and stone him to death." So the elders and nobles who lived in Naboth's city did as Jezebel directed in the letters she had written to them. They proclaimed a fast and seated Naboth in a prominent place among the people. Then two scoundrels came and sat opposite him and brought charges against Naboth before the people, saying, "Naboth has cursed both God and the king." So they took him outside the city and stoned him to death. Then they sent word to Jezebel: "Naboth has been stoned to death." (1 Kings 21:1–14 NIV)

Yesterday, we examined the importance of obedience to God and his will. Today, we will continue this concept but add to it the notion of finding the right people.

We have people who will guide us and ensure we get what we want. Especially in a discernment process, it is vital to ensure that those people won't simply give us what we want because we're whining. If we get to a place of whining, there is a good chance we're seeking to do what we want, rather than what God desires.

Today, I challenge you to find two or three people and have what I like to call *holy conversations*. (You likely already have talked with different people about your decision, so you don't need to repeat that.) The holy conversations are to help ensure you're not whining or trying to push your way to get what you want because you want it. This is why you need to pay attention to the voices you're listening to and the ears you bend when you need to talk.

You're probably getting antsy to make a decision and act on it. Remember, you need to make sure you're seeking God so that you will do the following:

- Become the person you need to be (and not a distorted image of who God desires and is making you to be).
- Trust that God is providing along the way.

- Pay attention to the movement and voice of God.
- Make sure you spend time connecting with God.
- Make sure you have the right people in your life to guide you to follow God and his will, instead of your selfish desires, who will make you stop whining.

If you are getting weary from this process, I encourage you to continue. Even if you believe you have already made a decision, tune in to the voice of God. You never know what will open up if you follow his lead, instead of pushing your way through to get something that may or may not be your best interest for God's kingdom.

Let's pray: Lord Jesus, guide me, and reveal yourself and your direction to me.

WESLEY COVENANT PRAYER

I am no longer my own, but yours.
Put me to what you will,
rank me with whom you will;
put me to doing,
put me to suffering;
let me be employed for you,
or laid aside for you,
exalted for you,
or brought low for you;
let me be full, let me be empty,
let me have all things,
let me have nothing:
I freely and wholeheartedly yield all things
to your pleasure and disposal.
And now, glorious and blessed God,
Father, Son and Holy Spirit,
you are mine and I am yours.

So be it.
And the covenant now made on earth,
let it be ratified in heaven.
Amen.

DAILY REFLECTION

Write about what God has revealed about himself. How is it with
your soul, just sitting in the presence of God? What is going through
your mind and heart about the decision or choice you need to make?

As soon as Jezebel heard that Naboth had been stoned to death, she said to Ahab, "Get up and take possession of the vineyard of Naboth the Jezreelite that he refused to sell you. He is no longer alive, but dead." When Ahab heard that Naboth was dead, he got up and went down to take possession of Naboth's vineyard. Then the word of the Lord came to Elijah the Tishbite: "Go down to meet Ahab king of Israel, who rules in Samaria. He is now in Naboth's vineyard, where he has gone to take possession of it. Say to him, 'This is what the Lord says: Have you not murdered a man and seized his property?' Then say to him, 'This is what the Lord says: In the place where dogs licked up Naboth's blood, dogs will lick up your blood—yes, yours!'"
(1 Kings 21:15–19 NIV)

Today, we get to a place where we can understand why we have been taking our time, discerning what to do next and ensuring that we are in step with God. There are consequences for doing things in our own time and in our own way. We may not have "dogs lick up [our] blood," but we may not be living life to the fullest and, therefore, we may feel as if we are being punished.

The point? As we step into the next steps, God requires that we count the cost (see Luke 14:25–35).

Much of this journey may seem like overkill, but we are making sure we're ready for the next stage of life. Today requires something more of us.

We've already discussed the spiritual disciplines of solitude and fasting. Today, we'll combine these two practices.

Challenge: Find some time to be alone. In this alone time, sit in silence, asking God to speak. The silence (and solitude) may once again feel odd and uncomfortable, so remember to rebuke any enemy that keeps you from hearing from God and God alone.

The goal is to find a minimum of fifteen to thirty minutes to be in solitude and silence. Allow yourself enough time to clear your head and be open to whatever God reveals.

If you are interested in learning more about *centering prayer* (what you're doing today), check out the book *Centering Prayer: Sitting Quietly in God's Presence Can Change Your Life* by Brian D. Russell.

While practicing this time of centering prayer in solitude, be sure to fast. This fast today can be from food, your phone, a television show, and so forth. Whatever you fast from, ask God to fill the void:

- Lord, I am hungry for food, but I know I am hungrier to hear from you.
- Lord, I know my phone helps me to connect with the world, and I may miss out on stuff, but help me connect to you deeply so that I rest and am content in your presence.
- Lord, I enjoy this show because it helps me calm down, but help me to understand how you bring true peace and calmness to my life.

This exercise may require you to remember what you experienced internally and what God said. Be sure to record with a journal (or write in this book) so that you can remember and reflect over the coming days and weeks.

God is with you and is guiding you to be his vessel and instrument to a world that needs to hear the message he gave you. Seek him to live out and speak out to those you encounter. Whatever path you ultimately decide will have consequences and also will give you opportunities to make an impact for the kingdom of God.

Let's pray: Lord Jesus, guide me, and reveal yourself and your direction to me.

WESLEY COVENANT PRAYER

I am no longer my own, but yours.
Put me to what you will,
rank me with whom you will;
put me to doing,
put me to suffering;
let me be employed for you,
or laid aside for you,
exalted for you,
or brought low for you;
let me be full, let me be empty,
let me have all things,
let me have nothing:
I freely and wholeheartedly yield all things
to your pleasure and disposal.
And now, glorious and blessed God,
Father, Son and Holy Spirit,
you are mine and I am yours.
So be it.
And the covenant now made on earth,
let it be ratified in heaven.
Amen.

DAILY REFLECTION

Write about what God has revealed about himself. How is it with your soul, just sitting in the presence of God? What is going through your mind and heart about the decision or choice you need to make?

Ahab said to Elijah, "So you have found me, my enemy!" "I have found you," he answered, "because you have sold yourself to do evil in the eyes of the Lord. He says, 'I am going to bring disaster on you. I will wipe out your descendants and cut off from Ahab every last male in Israel—slave or free. I will make your house like that of Jeroboam son of Nebat and that of Baasha son of Ahijah, because you have aroused my anger and have caused Israel to sin.' "And also concerning Jezebel the Lord says: 'Dogs will devour Jezebel by the wall of Jezreel.' "Dogs will eat those belonging to Ahab who die in the city, and the birds will feed on those who die in the country." (There was never anyone like Ahab, who sold himself to do evil in the eyes of the Lord, urged on by Jezebel his wife. He behaved in the vilest manner by going after idols, like the Amorites the Lord drove out before Israel.) (1 Kings 21:20–26 NIV)

Today, pay attention to the enemies you have or will encounter. Of course, these enemies could be people, but there is also a great chance you'll have other, more subtle enemies. The good news? God is capable of destroying all of the enemies you face.

I would challenge you to live in the *victory* that God has already provided and the way in which he works in and through you to bring light and hope to the world. If you live any other way, there is a chance you are worshipping and giving more attention to idols (false gods) than to the living God.

There is a path forward. There is hope because God is always moving you forward.

Ask God which enemies are in your way. Is it pride? Is it greed? Is it worshipping the past? Is it trying to be bigger and better than you are? Is it out of prejudice or misunderstanding or misinformation? What are your enemies? What do they whisper in your ear?

Look at the enemies that prevent you from fully living into God's hopeful and fruitful future. Then, ask God to reveal how these enemies have been destroyed so you can move forward.

Let's pray: Lord Jesus, guide me, and reveal yourself and your direction to me.

WESLEY COVENANT PRAYER

I am no longer my own, but yours.
Put me to what you will,
rank me with whom you will;
put me to doing,
put me to suffering;
let me be employed for you,
or laid aside for you,
exalted for you,
or brought low for you;
let me be full, let me be empty,
let me have all things,
let me have nothing:
I freely and wholeheartedly yield all things
to your pleasure and disposal.
And now, glorious and blessed God,
Father, Son and Holy Spirit,
you are mine and I am yours.
So be it.

And the covenant now made on earth,
let it be ratified in heaven.
Amen.

DAILY REFLECTION

Write about what God has revealed about himself. How is it with your soul, just sitting in the presence of God? What is going through your mind and heart about the decision or choice you need to make?

> When Ahab heard these words, he tore his clothes,
> put on sackcloth and fasted. He lay in sackcloth and
> went around meekly. Then the word of the Lord
> came to Elijah the Tishbite: "Have you noticed how
> Ahab has humbled himself before me? Because he
> has humbled himself, I will not bring this disaster in
> his day, but I will bring it on his house in the days
> of his son." (1 Kings 21:27–29 NIV)

Throughout this journey, I hope you have noticed how God has shaped and formed you to handle what's ahead. This is why we have spent so much time seeking God's presence, as well as seeking the kind of person God desires us to be.

The passage today is about God saying he'll cease the physical disaster, but we can see how God stops the spiritual disaster when we seek him and only him. To be the best version of ourselves and to know where God is leading us, we need to seek God's presence constantly. This requires humbling ourselves.

We can't make room for the movement of God in our lives unless we humble (ground) ourselves before the living God. Humbling requires we lower ourselves and put God in the proper place. We don't try to make ourselves better than we are—we live the way God has made us to be.

Notice how the disaster would hit future generations. Yet in the process of humbling ourselves, we also seek the thriving of future generations. How? We teach them, and we put ourselves in the position of modeling the kind of person who is humble before God.

We don't do this so we can escape the pits of hell. Instead, we live a humble life before God so we can live the best life possible—the life that reflects God in the world.

As we continue on this forty-day journey, we constantly seek God. Ask God to help us to be the people he needs us to be with the decision that needs to be made. To move into the next phase, humbling ourselves before God is vital.

We can humble ourselves in several ways and remember we are dependent on God. One of the best ways is by fasting. Our challenge today is to fast for one or two meals (or something else that distracts us from the voice of God). Then, during our times of fasting, we will go back and reread the scriptures we've read so far or some psalms or a gospel, and we will ask God to help us live humble lives.

We can say, "God, I know I have relied on myself for so long. Help me to constantly and completely rely on you."

Let's pray: Lord Jesus, guide me, and reveal yourself and your direction to me.

WESLEY COVENANT PRAYER

I am no longer my own, but yours.
Put me to what you will,
rank me with whom you will;
put me to doing,
put me to suffering;
let me be employed for you,
or laid aside for you,
exalted for you,
or brought low for you;
let me be full, let me be empty,
let me have all things,
let me have nothing:
I freely and wholeheartedly yield all things
to your pleasure and disposal.
And now, glorious and blessed God,

Father, Son and Holy Spirit,
you are mine and I am yours.
So be it.
And the covenant now made on earth,
let it be ratified in heaven.
Amen.

DAILY REFLECTION

Write about what God has revealed about himself. How is it with your soul, just sitting in the presence of God? What is going through your mind and heart about the decision or choice you need to make?

DAY 27

For three years there was no war between Aram and Israel. But in the third year Jehoshaphat king of Judah went down to see the king of Israel. The king of Israel had said to his officials, "Don't you know that Ramoth Gilead belongs to us and yet we are doing nothing to retake it from the king of Aram?" So he asked Jehoshaphat, "Will you go with me to fight against Ramoth Gilead?" Jehoshaphat replied to the king of Israel, "I am as you are, my people as your people, my horses as your horses." But Jehoshaphat also said to the king of Israel, "First seek the counsel of the Lord." So the king of Israel brought together the prophets—about four hundred men—and asked them, "Shall I go to war against Ramoth Gilead, or shall I refrain?" "Go," they answered, "for the Lord will give it into the king's hand." But Jehoshaphat asked, "Is there no longer a prophet of the Lord here whom we can inquire of?" The king of Israel answered Jehoshaphat, "There is still one prophet through whom we can inquire of the Lord, but I hate him because he never prophesies anything good about me, but always bad. He is Micaiah son of Imlah." "The king should not say such a thing," Jehoshaphat replied. (1 Kings 22:1–8 NIV)

We have spent so much time focusing on seeking God's face and his will and on the kind of person we want to become after we discern which path to take next. Now we will look at a different angle of the discernment process.

You may feel sometimes as if everything depends on you, that you have to be the one to make the right decision. Please do not fall into that line of thinking—it is a trap! How? There are forces that will try to keep you isolated. Some mindsets can make you think that you don't need other people. Any of these situations will keep you from making the best decision possible.

What should you do? Take time to evaluate from whom you get counsel and to whom you give counsel.

We need each other. Humanity was never meant to make decisions alone and live a life isolated from others. We were meant to live in a community.

Today, your task is simple. Write down the names of the people you trust. These should not be only the people who think like you and who will say whatever you want to help you feel better. No. These names must be those people who are willing to tell you the truth, tell it in love, and show you they are praying for you. Yes, we have thought about names of people before. This step helps make seeking their input more concrete.

These people also will direct you to continue to seek the Lord. If you don't have these people, your support network in the future will be lacking. You may be dealing with a big decision right now, but be wary of trying to handle it alone.

You've been doing some soul-searching. This work will continue throughout your life. As you seek the Lord, also seek the people who will be truth-tellers to help you see the bigger picture, who will help you see things you may not have seen.

Let's pray: Lord Jesus, guide me, and reveal yourself and your direction to me.

WESLEY COVENANT PRAYER

I am no longer my own, but yours.
Put me to what you will,
rank me with whom you will;
put me to doing,
put me to suffering;
let me be employed for you,
or laid aside for you,
exalted for you,
or brought low for you;
let me be full, let me be empty,
let me have all things,
let me have nothing:
I freely and wholeheartedly yield all things
to your pleasure and disposal.
And now, glorious and blessed God,
Father, Son and Holy Spirit,
you are mine and I am yours.
So be it.
And the covenant now made on earth,
let it be ratified in heaven.
Amen.

DAY 28 REFLECTION

Today is a day of Sabbath rest. Use this day to connect with and praise God, and reflect on how you have experienced God in this past week.

Read: Psalm 8

Reflect: How have you experienced God's grace in this past week? How has God changed you over the past month?

Let's pray: Lord Jesus, guide me, and reveal yourself and your direction to me.

WESLEY COVENANT PRAYER

I am no longer my own, but yours.
Put me to what you will,
rank me with whom you will;
put me to doing,
put me to suffering;
let me be employed for you,
or laid aside for you,
exalted for you,
or brought low for you;
let me be full, let me be empty,
let me have all things,
let me have nothing:
I freely and wholeheartedly yield all things
to your pleasure and disposal.
And now, glorious and blessed God,

Father, Son and Holy Spirit,
you are mine and I am yours.
So be it.
And the covenant now made on earth,
let it be ratified in heaven.
Amen.

So the king of Israel called one of his officials and said, "Bring Micaiah son of Imlah at once." Dressed in their royal robes, the king of Israel and Jehoshaphat king of Judah were sitting on their thrones at the threshing floor by the entrance of the gate of Samaria, with all the prophets prophesying before them. Now Zedekiah son of Kenaanah had made iron horns and he declared, "This is what the Lord says: 'With these you will gore the Arameans until they are destroyed.'" All the other prophets were prophesying the same thing. "Attack Ramoth Gilead and be victorious," they said, "for the Lord will give it into the king's hand." The messenger who had gone to summon Micaiah said to him, "Look, the other prophets without exception are predicting success for the king. Let your word agree with theirs, and speak favorably." But Micaiah said, "As surely as the Lord lives, I can tell him only what the Lord tells me." When he arrived, the king asked him, "Micaiah, shall we go to war against Ramoth Gilead, or not?" "Attack and be victorious," he answered, "for the Lord will give it into the king's hand." The king said to him, "How many times must I make you swear to tell me nothing but the truth in the name of the Lord?" Then Micaiah answered, "I saw all Israel scattered on the hills like sheep without a shepherd, and the Lord said, 'These people have no master. Let each one go home in peace.'" The king of Israel said to Jehoshaphat,

"Didn't I tell you that he never prophesies anything good about me, but only bad?" Micaiah continued, "Therefore hear the word of the Lord: I saw the Lord sitting on his throne with all the multitudes of heaven standing around him on his right and on his left. And the Lord said, 'Who will entice Ahab into attacking Ramoth Gilead and going to his death there?' "One suggested this, and another that. Finally, a spirit came forward, stood before the Lord and said, 'I will entice him.' "'By what means?' the Lord asked. "'I will go out and be a deceiving spirit in the mouths of all his prophets,' he said. "'You will succeed in enticing him,' said the Lord. 'Go and do it.' "So now the Lord has put a deceiving spirit in the mouths of all these prophets of yours. The Lord has decreed disaster for you." (1 Kings 22:9–23 NIV)

As we near the end of the forty days, you may feel good about your decision, or you still may be conflicted. The main thing is this: always make sure you are seeking God and God alone. Otherwise, you may find you are stepping out on our own, rather than in God's direction.

A few days ago, we talked about the importance of having the right people as our counsel. The people with whom we surround ourselves with will encourage us forward or pull us down. Again, we need people who will tell us the truth, rather than just tickling our ears to make us feel good.

King Ahab liked his prophets because they told him what he wanted to hear, but he could not stand Micaiah because Micaiah would not always speak favorably to the king. The king refused to listen to anything except what he wanted to hear.

We need people to speak the truth to us, and we need to listen, even when it hurts our feelings. Our feelings will heal, and we'll also find our character is better and stronger. Will God be with us after we make our decisions? The answer is yes.

You might make decisions based on what you think will give you an easier life or what you want to hear because it makes you feel good. God is always more concerned with your holiness (wholeness or completeness) than your happiness. Happiness is fleeting, but the joy of following and living in the truth is much more sustainable.

From here on out, do what the apostle Paul says in 1 Thessalonians 5: "Do not quench the Spirit. Do not treat prophecies with contempt but test them all; hold on to what is good."

The "good" you should seek to keep is from God. Make sure what you hear lines up with God through the scriptures. Test what others say to see if their words are beneficial for building God's kingdom.

Always live in the truth, knowing it is the best thing for you.

Let's pray: Lord Jesus, guide me, and reveal yourself and your direction to me.

WESLEY COVENANT PRAYER

I am no longer my own, but yours.
Put me to what you will,
rank me with whom you will;
put me to doing,
put me to suffering;
let me be employed for you,
or laid aside for you,
exalted for you,
or brought low for you;
let me be full, let me be empty,
let me have all things,
let me have nothing:
I freely and wholeheartedly yield all things
to your pleasure and disposal.

And now, glorious and blessed God,
Father, Son and Holy Spirit,
you are mine and I am yours.
So be it.
And the covenant now made on earth,
let it be ratified in heaven.
Amen.

DAILY REFLECTION

Write about what God has revealed about himself. How is it with your soul, just sitting in the presence of God? What is going through your mind and heart about the decision or choice you need to make?

Then Zedekiah son of Kenaanah went up and slapped Micaiah in the face. "Which way did the spirit from the Lord go when he went from me to speak to you?" he asked. Micaiah replied, "You will find out on the day you go to hide in an inner room." The king of Israel then ordered, "Take Micaiah and send him back to Amon the ruler of the city and to Joash the king's son and say, 'This is what the king says: Put this fellow in prison and give him nothing but bread and water until I return safely.'" Micaiah declared, "If you ever return safely, the Lord has not spoken through me." Then he added, "Mark my words, all you people!" So the king of Israel and Jehoshaphat king of Judah went up to Ramoth Gilead. The king of Israel said to Jehoshaphat, "I will enter the battle in disguise, but you wear your royal robes." So the king of Israel disguised himself and went into battle. Now the king of Aram had ordered his thirty-two chariot commanders, "Do not fight with anyone, small or great, except the king of Israel." When the chariot commanders saw Jehoshaphat, they thought, "Surely this is the king of Israel." So they turned to attack him, but when Jehoshaphat cried out, the chariot commanders saw that he was not the king of Israel and stopped pursuing him. But someone drew his bow at random and hit the king of Israel between the sections of his armor. The king told his chariot driver, "Wheel around and get me out of the fighting. I've been wounded." (1 Kings 22:24–34 NIV)

It is not always easy to do as the Lord directs and guides you. Some will not understand and will make fun of you or insult you for following the Lord's guidance.

But we have spent this time preparing ourselves to enter into the next steps that God has called for us. Taking the time to discern the next steps is vital so that the Lord can also strengthen us. For example, look at Jesus's baptism (Matthew 3) and his temptations in the wilderness (Matthew 4).

At first glance, we might assume that Jesus was weak and consumed with hunger after spending forty days fasting and praying. The reality, however, is that Jesus was at his strongest because (1) he was grounded in his identity, spoken at his baptism, and (2) he'd just spent forty days with the Holy Spirit filling him. Spending this intentional time with God is about being filled and strengthened to handle what comes next.

Rest is vital. When we devote ourselves entirely to resting in the presence of God and being strengthened by his Spirit, then we will use better judgment on what to do next. We won't make rash or quick decisions. Instead, our minds will have been shaped toward that of Jesus Christ.

What else happens after spending time with God? We will go out in the world as our authentic selves. We do not need to put on any disguise or fake personality. We will be grounded in who God says we are.

Today, spend time praising God for who he formed you to be. Praise God for the mind to discern (even if you're still deciding). Praise God for the gift of friends who keep you focused on God.

Praise God, especially when you're figuring things out. Why? Because you always can praise God because he is doing incredible work in and through you, preparing you for the next step forward.

Let's pray: Lord Jesus, guide me, and reveal yourself and your direction to me.

WESLEY COVENANT PRAYER

I am no longer my own, but yours.
Put me to what you will,
rank me with whom you will;
put me to doing,
put me to suffering;
let me be employed for you,
or laid aside for you,
exalted for you,
or brought low for you;
let me be full, let me be empty,
let me have all things,
let me have nothing:
I freely and wholeheartedly yield all things
to your pleasure and disposal.
And now, glorious and blessed God,
Father, Son and Holy Spirit,
you are mine and I am yours.
So be it.
And the covenant now made on earth,
let it be ratified in heaven.
Amen.

DAILY REFLECTION

Write about what God has revealed about himself. How is it with your soul, just sitting in the presence of God? What is going through your mind and heart about the decision or choice you need to make?

All day long the battle raged, and the king was propped up in his chariot facing the Arameans. The blood from his wound ran onto the floor of the chariot, and that evening he died. As the sun was setting, a cry spread through the army: "Every man to his town. Every man to his land!" So the king died and was brought to Samaria, and they buried him there. They washed the chariot at a pool in Samaria (where the prostitutes bathed), and the dogs licked up his blood, as the word of the Lord had declared. As for the other events of Ahab's reign, including all he did, the palace he built and adorned with ivory, and the cities he fortified, are they not written in the book of the annals of the kings of Israel? Ahab rested with his ancestors. And Ahaziah his son succeeded him as king. Jehoshaphat son of Asa became king of Judah in the fourth year of Ahab king of Israel. (1 Kings 22:35–41 NIV)

There will come the point when the battle over which decision to make will be done. At some point, you must decide and stick with it. If you already have made up your mind and feel this is the path on which God is leading you, that's perfect! I still encourage you to finish this discernment process for the final days. Why? Because the point is to ensure that you seek God and not just what you want. It is about allowing the Spirit of God to transform your heart and mind for what he has planned next.

Don't worry or fret if you are still trying to make a decision. Keep trusting that the answer will be revealed in God's time. Hold fast and strong to what you have experienced so far while you've been in the presence of God and always find ways to praise him.

Today, we will sit still and try to remember what God has told us over the last month. This time has not been wasted, but, as the Word of the Lord was fulfilled to Ahab, God's Word to you is not empty. God will keep what he has said. Trust him.

So, we sit. We remember. We make sure that what we have heard from God aligns with scripture and not just what we want. It's not that God won't give us what we want; it's more that God is making sure to provide for us, based on who we are and who we will become.

There are no quick fixes. There are no shortcuts. God is working and is preparing you to be his person for the next season. You never know—there might be something in the way right now. You must wait before stepping into the next season. Jehoshaphat had to wait until Ahab was out of the picture.

If we try to move before God is ready, we may find ourselves in the way.

Let's pray: Lord Jesus, guide me, and reveal yourself and your direction to me.

WESLEY COVENANT PRAYER

I am no longer my own, but yours.
Put me to what you will,
rank me with whom you will;
put me to doing,
put me to suffering;
let me be employed for you,
or laid aside for you,
exalted for you,
or brought low for you;
let me be full, let me be empty,
let me have all things,
let me have nothing:

I freely and wholeheartedly yield all things
to your pleasure and disposal.
And now, glorious and blessed God,
Father, Son and Holy Spirit,
you are mine and I am yours.
So be it.
And the covenant now made on earth,
let it be ratified in heaven.
Amen.

DAILY REFLECTION

Write about what God has revealed about himself. How is it with
your soul, just sitting in the presence of God? What is going through
your mind and heart about the decision or choice you need to make?`

Jehoshaphat was thirty-five years old when he became king, and he reigned in Jerusalem twenty-five years. His mother's name was Azubah daughter of Shilhi. In everything he followed the ways of his father Asa and did not stray from them; he did what was right in the eyes of the Lord. The high places, however, were not removed, and the people continued to offer sacrifices and burn incense there. Jehoshaphat was also at peace with the king of Israel. As for the other events of Jehoshaphat's reign, the things he achieved and his military exploits, are they not written in the book of the annals of the kings of Judah? He rid the land of the rest of the male shrine prostitutes who remained there even after the reign of his father Asa. There was then no king in Edom; a provincial governor ruled. (1 Kings 22:42–47 NIV)

As we draw this time of discernment to a close, you may fall into one of three categories:

1. You feel ready to move forward.
2. You still haven't decided.
3. You know what to do, but you're not quite ready to move forward.

Don't worry; this is not a time to stress. Instead, this is a time to see how your life has been shaped and cleaned out before moving forward in your decision. We have focused much more on who God is than on which decision to make because without the grounding of who God is and who God says you are, you can easily miss out on being the person God is asking you be in this next phase.

Today, we will do something we have done before: we will analyze to whom we listen. In other words, do we simply follow the ways of our parents or other significant figure(s)? Or do we do everything we can to eliminate all other voices except that of God?

Hebrews 3:15 is a reminder for me every day: "Today, if you hear his voice, do not harden your hearts." If we try to keep past successes and ways of living in our paths and in our everyday lives, they will come back to haunt us, tempt us, and cause us to fall. The pull of these idols is too great for us, and we'll find ourselves in a situation where nothing about us has genuinely changed.

Therefore, we are taking the time to rid our lives of *anything* that does not keep our focus and attention on God. We do not need to be concerned if these idols are not removed today. This will be a process. It will take time to dismantle them and allow the Holy Spirit to foster a new dependency on him, rather than old rituals.

How can the power of t our old idols be removed? First, find someone you trust to help you. Then, talk with a counselor or pastor to help you release the hold of these idols. You are moving into a new phase, and the presence of the living God is transforming you.

Whatever your decision, these idols need to be removed because they will impede your walk in the next phase.

Read and meditate on the following:

> Therefore, I urge you, brothers and sisters, in view of God's mercy, to offer your bodies as a living sacrifice, holy and pleasing to God—this is your true and proper worship. Do not conform to the pattern of this world, but be transformed by the renewing of your mind. Then you will be able to test and approve what God's will is—his good, pleasing and perfect will. (Romans 12:1–2 NIV)

Let's pray: Lord Jesus, guide me, and reveal yourself and your direction to me.

WESLEY COVENANT PRAYER

I am no longer my own, but yours.
Put me to what you will,
rank me with whom you will;
put me to doing,
put me to suffering;
let me be employed for you,
or laid aside for you,
exalted for you,
or brought low for you;
let me be full, let me be empty,
let me have all things,
let me have nothing:
I freely and wholeheartedly yield all things
to your pleasure and disposal.
And now, glorious and blessed God,
Father, Son and Holy Spirit,
you are mine and I am yours.
So be it.
And the covenant now made on earth,
let it be ratified in heaven.
Amen.

DAILY REFLECTION

Write about what God has revealed about himself. How is it with your soul, just sitting in the presence of God? What is going through your mind and heart about the decision or choice you need to make?

Now Jehoshaphat built a fleet of trading ships to go to Ophir for gold, but they never set sail—they were wrecked at Ezion Geber. At that time Ahaziah son of Ahab said to Jehoshaphat, "Let my men sail with yours," but Jehoshaphat refused. Then Jehoshaphat rested with his ancestors and was buried with them in the city of David his father. And Jehoram his son succeeded him as king. Ahaziah son of Ahab became king of Israel in Samaria in the seventeenth year of Jehoshaphat king of Judah, and he reigned over Israel two years. He did evil in the eyes of the Lord, because he followed the ways of his father and mother and of Jeroboam son of Nebat, who caused Israel to sin. He served and worshiped Baal and aroused the anger of the Lord, the God of Israel, just as his father had done. (1 Kings 22:48–53 NIV)

Notice the contrast in this passage between Jehoshaphat and Ahaziah. Each one followed the ways of his father. Each one lived according to certain patterns that were handed down to him. One set of patterns brought prosperity and harmony; the other was evil, against God and his will.

As we prepare to enter the next phase, look at the patterns you live by. How do you structure your day? How do you interact with others? What is your information source?

We need to evaluate these points because whatever decision we make, we cannot live in the same manner as before. When we make a life-changing decision, we don't just put our current selves in a new position; this is an opportunity to live a little differently.

We evaluate our life patterns to make sure they are and will be in line with what we're going to do next.

Why is this part of the discernment process? It is because whatever decision we make, we will be changed and affected by it. We need to make sure we're becoming the person we want to be and that we will stick with our convictions.

God may have given us an opportunity to live differently, to refocus on him, and to be truly transformed into the image of his Son, Jesus Christ.

Why would we think we can be the same moving forward as we have been in the past? Again, we need to evaluate this over time.

Beginning today, look at your habits, convictions, and routines, and see if they align with what you'll be doing and where you're going next.

Remember, you have been given this opportunity to see how God is shaping you to become his person in this world, to shine his light so the world can see, and to share and show the kingdom of God all around you. There are many opportunities ahead. Allow God to shape and form you so you'll be the best version of yourself—not just to survive but thrive!

Read and mediate on Colossians 3:1–17 today.

Let's pray: Lord Jesus, guide me, and reveal yourself and your direction to me.

WESLEY COVENANT PRAYER

I am no longer my own, but yours.
Put me to what you will,
rank me with whom you will;
put me to doing,
put me to suffering;
let me be employed for you,
or laid aside for you,
exalted for you,

or brought low for you;
let me be full, let me be empty,
let me have all things,
let me have nothing:
I freely and wholeheartedly yield all things
to your pleasure and disposal.
And now, glorious and blessed God,
Father, Son and Holy Spirit,
you are mine and I am yours.
So be it.
And the covenant now made on earth,
let it be ratified in heaven.
Amen.

DAILY REFLECTION

Write about what God has revealed about himself. How is it with
your soul, just sitting in the presence of God? What is going through
your mind and heart about the decision or choice you need to make?

After Ahab's death, Moab rebelled against Israel.
Now Ahaziah had fallen through the lattice of his
upper room in Samaria and injured himself. So he
sent messengers, saying to them, "Go and consult
Baal-Zebub, the god of Ekron, to see if I will recover
from this injury." But the angel of the Lord said to
Elijah the Tishbite, "Go up and meet the messengers
of the king of Samaria and ask them, 'Is it because
there is no God in Israel that you are going off to
consult Baal-Zebub, the god of Ekron?' Therefore
this is what the Lord says: 'You will not leave the
bed you are lying on. You will certainly die!'" So
Elijah went. When the messengers returned to the
king, he asked them, "Why have you come back?"
"A man came to meet us," they replied. "And he said
to us, 'Go back to the king who sent you and tell
him, "This is what the Lord says: Is it because there
is no God in Israel that you are sending messengers
to consult Baal-Zebub, the god of Ekron? Therefore
you will not leave the bed you are lying on. You
will certainly die!"'" The king asked them, "What
kind of man was it who came to meet you and
told you this?" They replied, "He had a garment of
hair and had a leather belt around his waist." The
king said, "That was Elijah the Tishbite." (2 Kings
1:1–8 NIV)

What will you be, and what are you known for? We gave these
questions today. Whatever decision you must make, it is essential

to go back and ask yourself, "What am I known for?" Why should you ask this question? Because unless there is a change for the better, everything will remain the same, but you will be put in a different position.

As I see it, one big reason why people don't succeed in a new area is that they haven't adapted to the new organization, job, school, or vacation. Meaning, the person has not changed. The person is still operating in a manner that they have done before and have not made the changes necessary. The challenge comes in when we try to please other people, or try to be who we think others want us to be. This is why it's important to know who God is and who you are. Without being firm in God's identity, you will falter but not understand why.

The world will keep changing. Chaos will follow wherever you go. There is no way to escape what's happening in the world, and a new position or placement will not change anything, except where you happen to be.

Elijah must have been a sight to see, but his focus was on doing the will and directives of God. It did not matter that his clothing made him stand out. What mattered was his devotion. He was the person God used in different situations to deliver hard truths to Israel's kings. He could do this because the power of God was with him and because he kept his life in alignment with God.

Elijah was able to be the person God needed him to be in different situations because Elijah was open to the movement of the Spirit, transforming him and giving him what he needed to handle whatever was ahead.

Today, fast and pray. Ask God how you will be changed after the decision is made. Then, ask God to help you accept the changes and to ensure you are ready to become that person.

> My son, do not forget my teaching, but keep my
> commands in your heart, for they will prolong your
> life many years and bring you peace and prosperity.
> Let love and faithfulness never leave you; bind them

around your neck, write them on the tablet of your heart. Then you will win favor and a good name in the sight of God and man. Trust in the Lord with all your heart and lean not on your own understanding; in all your ways submit to him, and he will make your paths straight. (Proverbs 3:1–6 NIV)

Let's pray: Lord Jesus, guide me, and reveal yourself and your direction to me.

WESLEY COVENANT PRAYER

I am no longer my own, but yours.
Put me to what you will,
rank me with whom you will;
put me to doing,
put me to suffering;
let me be employed for you,
or laid aside for you,
exalted for you,
or brought low for you;
let me be full, let me be empty,
let me have all things,
let me have nothing:
I freely and wholeheartedly yield all things
to your pleasure and disposal.
And now, glorious and blessed God,
Father, Son and Holy Spirit,
you are mine and I am yours.
So be it.
And the covenant now made on earth,
let it be ratified in heaven.
Amen.

DAILY REFLECTION

Write about what God has revealed about himself. How is it with your soul, just sitting in the presence of God? What is going through your mind and heart about the decision or choice you need to make?

Today is a day of Sabbath rest. Use this day to connect with and praise God, and reflect on how you have experienced God in this past week.

Read: Psalm 65

Reflect: How have you experienced God's grace in this past week? What do you believe God is leading you to do?

Let's pray: Lord Jesus, guide me, and reveal yourself and your direction to me.

WESLEY COVENANT PRAYER

I am no longer my own, but yours.
Put me to what you will,
rank me with whom you will;
put me to doing,
put me to suffering;
let me be employed for you,
or laid aside for you,
exalted for you,
or brought low for you;
let me be full, let me be empty,
let me have all things,
let me have nothing:
I freely and wholeheartedly yield all things
to your pleasure and disposal.
And now, glorious and blessed God,

Father, Son and Holy Spirit,
you are mine and I am yours.
So be it.
And the covenant now made on earth,
let it be ratified in heaven.
Amen.

Then he sent to Elijah a captain with his company of fifty men. The captain went up to Elijah, who was sitting on the top of a hill, and said to him, "Man of God, the king says, 'Come down!'" Elijah answered the captain, "If I am a man of God, may fire come down from heaven and consume you and your fifty men!" Then fire fell from heaven and consumed the captain and his men. At this the king sent to Elijah another captain with his fifty men. The captain said to him, "Man of God, this is what the king says, 'Come down at once!'" "If I am a man of God," Elijah replied, "may fire come down from heaven and consume you and your fifty men!" Then the fire of God fell from heaven and consumed him and his fifty men. So the king sent a third captain with his fifty men. This third captain went up and fell on his knees before Elijah. "Man of God," he begged, "please have respect for my life and the lives of these fifty men, your servants! See, fire has fallen from heaven and consumed the first two captains and all their men. But now have respect for my life!" (2 Kings 1:9–14 NIV)

As we move into a new direction, a new phase, we have to talk about confidence versus arrogance.

Arrogance is doing things and living in such a way (especially in communication with others) that makes you seem better than you might be. Arrogance stems from pride, and pride will cause you to stumble and fall.

Confidence, and we are describing it here, is a deep trust in God—who God is, who God says we are, and what God can do. Confidence means you can be assertive yet humble. Confidence is the key.

We've discussed living in a way that glorifies God, and living in confidence is the way to live.

Look at Elijah.

He was confident that God would hear him. He was confident God would move. He was confident God would reveal himself. That's the kind of confidence we should live by every day. Our decisions are important to God. Although God will work through any decision we make, we have the opportunity to live in confidence and deep trust—or we can become persons who do not give God the glory.

All of life is truly about God and how we live. God is moving us in a new direction. Even if that direction means we do not make a move, we will be different because God has transformed us inside and out.

There are four more days in this discernment process. I encourage you to continue strong. You may feel as if you already know what to do, but there still may be work God needs to do in and through you before moving forward.

You still need to cultivate the habit of resting in and trusting God through the gift of faith that God has bestowed upon you.

QUESTIONS

How confident are you in your abilities and gifts?

How confident are you that God is with you and will provide each day?

Does the confidence you have inspire others, or does it drive people away?

Let's pray: Lord Jesus, guide me, and reveal yourself and your direction to me.

WESLEY COVENANT PRAYER

I am no longer my own, but yours.
Put me to what you will,
rank me with whom you will;
put me to doing,
put me to suffering;
let me be employed for you,
or laid aside for you,
exalted for you,
or brought low for you;
let me be full, let me be empty,
let me have all things,
let me have nothing:
I freely and wholeheartedly yield all things
to your pleasure and disposal.
And now, glorious and blessed God,
Father, Son and Holy Spirit,
you are mine and I am yours.
So be it.
And the covenant now made on earth,
let it be ratified in heaven.
Amen.

DAILY REFLECTION

Write about what God has revealed about himself. How is it with your soul, just sitting in the presence of God? What is going through your mind and heart about the decision or choice you need to make?

The angel of the Lord said to Elijah, "Go down with him; do not be afraid of him." So Elijah got up and went down with him to the king. He told the king, "This is what the Lord says: Is it because there is no God in Israel for you to consult that you have sent messengers to consult Baal-Zebub, the god of Ekron? Because you have done this, you will never leave the bed you are lying on. You will certainly die!" So he died, according to the word of the Lord that Elijah had spoken. Because Ahaziah had no son, Joram succeeded him as king in the second year of Jehoram son of Jehoshaphat king of Judah. As for all the other events of Ahaziah's reign, and what he did, are they not written in the book of the annals of the kings of Israel? (2 Kings 1:15–18 NIV)

The phrase "do not be afraid" is interesting. Fear can keep us safe from something dangerous. Fear can also hinder us from doing what we need to do.

Consider this:

1. Ask yourself what you are afraid of, especially when it comes to deciding or living into your decision.
2. Realize that whatever you fear is ultimately what you worship.

Let me reiterate that second point: whatever we fear is ultimately what we worship, what we give our attention and focus. We will do whatever is necessary to keep our fears at bay. We will feed our fears with stories. We will allow our fears to stop us from doing things. We will be driven toward fear so that we live with the sensationalism we crave, which means we keep returning to what makes us fearful which may lead us further from God's desire for our lives.

The point? Scripture repeatedly says "do not be afraid." The scriptures *also* say, "Fear only God." Why? Because if we fear God, then we'll worship him.

Fearing God is not a paralyzing fear. On the contrary, it is a deep reverence for who God is and what God says. It is a deep longing to know God and to stay on the path God desires for us. It is about not becoming less than who he created us to be. Fear is when we are afraid *not* to follow his Word.

As you step into this next cycle after your decision, keep paying attention to what you fear. Notice what drives you. You may find that what you fear is what drives you. If you're driven by success, money, prominence, and so forth, then you may need to check yourself because you should have a desire to please and serve God and God alone. You should be fearful of what can happen when you don't follow him.

You always should ask yourself this question: do I seek to serve and follow God, or do I seek to satisfy my desires for comfort, a new situation, and so on?

You must understand and remember each day that God is with you. God is working in and through you. God is doing everything he can to make himself known in and through your life. Remember that in whatever decision you make, leave room for God to work and reveal himself through the next phase you'll enter. Then, when it's time, step out without fear or reservation.

Let's pray: Lord Jesus, guide me, and reveal yourself and your direction to me.

WESLEY COVENANT PRAYER

I am no longer my own, but yours.
Put me to what you will,
rank me with whom you will;
put me to doing,
put me to suffering;
let me be employed for you,
or laid aside for you,
exalted for you,
or brought low for you;
let me be full, let me be empty,
let me have all things,
let me have nothing:
I freely and wholeheartedly yield all things
to your pleasure and disposal.
And now, glorious and blessed God,
Father, Son and Holy Spirit,
you are mine and I am yours.
So be it.
And the covenant now made on earth,
let it be ratified in heaven.
Amen.

DAILY REFLECTION

Write about what God has revealed about himself. How is it with your soul, just sitting in the presence of God? What is going through your mind and heart about the decision or choice you need to make?

When the Lord was about to take Elijah up to heaven in a whirlwind, Elijah and Elisha were on their way from Gilgal. Elijah said to Elisha, "Stay here; the Lord has sent me to Bethel." But Elisha said, "As surely as the Lord lives and as you live, I will not leave you." So they went down to Bethel. The company of the prophets at Bethel came out to Elisha and asked, "Do you know that the Lord is going to take your master from you today?" "Yes, I know," Elisha replied, "so be quiet." Then Elijah said to him, "Stay here, Elisha; the Lord has sent me to Jericho." And he replied, "As surely as the Lord lives and as you live, I will not leave you." So they went to Jericho. The company of the prophets at Jericho went up to Elisha and asked him, "Do you know that the Lord is going to take your master from you today?" "Yes, I know," he replied, "so be quiet." Then Elijah said to him, "Stay here; the Lord has sent me to the Jordan." And he replied, "As surely as the Lord lives and as you live, I will not leave you." So the two of them walked on. (2 Kings 2:1–6 NIV)

You have allowed God to prepare and transform you into the person he needs you to be. Soon, you will need to step out and do what the Lord has said.

Notice how Elisha will not leave Elijah's side. I am praying that you have someone who sticks that close to you to encourage you and move along with you in the next phase, after you make the decision. Why do you need this? Because we all need someone to encourage us. We cannot live life alone, nor do we ever go into any new situation alone.

God has brought people along our paths to help guide, nurture, and reflect his image to us. God also has brought people alongside us to learn from us. We have opportunities to show the full range of emotions and reality when we do something new. How we handle ourselves and trust in God's presence and gifts will be a great teachable moment for another person; God uses us for this.

Today, reflect upon who is taking this journey with you. Have you thanked them for their support? Their listening ears? The time they invested in ensuring you were listening to the voice of God? If you have thanked them, thank them again. Praise, especially praising God, always puts us on a trajectory of being more grateful and hopeful about what God is doing.

The other thing to notice is that God might be about to do incredible work. Perhaps the doors will swing open wide. Maybe you'll find more people in the same boat as you, or maybe you will wait longer. The point of this? Ask God to open your eyes to what he is doing, and ask him to reveal his workings to you.

After we complete this forty-day journey, continue to seek the presence of the living God and pay attention to how he is working in and through you for his kingdom's glory.

Let's pray: Lord Jesus, guide me, and reveal yourself and your direction to me.

WESLEY COVENANT PRAYER

I am no longer my own, but yours.
Put me to what you will,
rank me with whom you will;
put me to doing,
put me to suffering;
let me be employed for you,

or laid aside for you,
exalted for you,
or brought low for you;
let me be full, let me be empty,
let me have all things,
let me have nothing:
I freely and wholeheartedly yield all things
to your pleasure and disposal.
And now, glorious and blessed God,
Father, Son and Holy Spirit,
you are mine and I am yours.
So be it.
And the covenant now made on earth,
let it be ratified in heaven.
Amen.

DAILY REFLECTION

Write about what God has revealed about himself. How is it with your soul, just sitting in the presence of God? What is going through your mind and heart about the decision or choice you need to make?

> Fifty men from the company of the prophets went and stood at a distance, facing the place where Elijah and Elisha had stopped at the Jordan. Elijah took his cloak, rolled it up and struck the water with it. The water divided to the right and to the left, and the two of them crossed over on dry ground. When they had crossed, Elijah said to Elisha, "Tell me, what can I do for you before I am taken from you?" "Let me inherit a double portion of your spirit," Elisha replied. "You have asked a difficult thing," Elijah said, "yet if you see me when I am taken from you, it will be yours—otherwise, it will not."
> (2 Kings 2:7–10 NIV)

You may or may not feel the urgency to move forward with your decision. Nevertheless, today's passage invites you to pause, once again, to see what God has in store for you.

Elisha was traveling with Elijah. Elisha knew it was time for Elijah to depart, so he probably was nervous. His nerves probably caused anxiety and impatience. He wanted to know exactly what was going to happen.

Here's the deal: we all get impatient with God because it seems like he is taking his time. We can feel that God is late, but is he? Or does God know the best timing, and his timing just doesn't fit into the human conception of time?

Elisha had left everything to follow Elijah, and he wanted what Elijah had—being able to do the same things as Elijah did would be pretty cool. But Elijah kept insisting that Elisha still had some stuff to do and work on. Elisha needed to work on patience. Elisha needed to work on seeing what he was supposed to see.

I think we often jump off the deep end when we make decisions because we think we have thought about it from every angle, and we know what to expect. But do we? Or are we still trying to move in our own way and in our own strength?

What if God is constantly working on our level of patience? What if God asks us to move but not in the speed or manner we want to go?

Today is a day to ask God if you are ready to move forward. Today, you are invited to pause and listen. Go back to doing the centering-prayer exercise we did earlier. Find some time to be in solitude and quiet. Try to clear your head and listen. Simply listen.

Always move forward with the presence of God and trust that he is transforming you to become the person he needs for your next step.

Patience and trust and vision are essential. Ask God to help you grow in these areas; then, be prepared to watch God work, and be ready when God says *go*!

Let's pray: Lord Jesus, guide me, and reveal yourself and your direction to me.

WESLEY COVENANT PRAYER

I am no longer my own, but yours.
Put me to what you will,
rank me with whom you will;
put me to doing,
put me to suffering;
let me be employed for you,
or laid aside for you,
exalted for you,
or brought low for you;
let me be full, let me be empty,

let me have all things,
let me have nothing:
I freely and wholeheartedly yield all things
to your pleasure and disposal.
And now, glorious and blessed God,
Father, Son and Holy Spirit,
you are mine and I am yours.
So be it.
And the covenant now made on earth,
let it be ratified in heaven.
Amen.

DAILY REFLECTION

Write about what God has revealed about himself. How is it with your soul, just sitting in the presence of God? What is going through your mind and heart about the decision or choice you need to make?

DAY 40

As they were walking along and talking together, suddenly a chariot of fire and horses of fire appeared and separated the two of them, and Elijah went up to heaven in a whirlwind. Elisha saw this and cried out, "My father! My father! The chariots and horsemen of Israel!" And Elisha saw him no more. Then he took hold of his garment and tore it in two. Elisha then picked up Elijah's cloak that had fallen from him and went back and stood on the bank of the Jordan. He took the cloak that had fallen from Elijah and struck the water with it. "Where now is the Lord, the God of Elijah?" he asked. When he struck the water, it divided to the right and to the left, and he crossed over. The company of the prophets from Jericho, who were watching, said, "The spirit of Elijah is resting on Elisha." And they went to meet him and bowed to the ground before him. "Look," they said, "we your servants have fifty able men. Let them go and look for your master. Perhaps the Spirit of the Lord has picked him up and set him down on some mountain or in some valley." "No," Elisha replied, "do not send them." But they persisted until he was too embarrassed to refuse. So he said, "Send them." And they sent fifty men, who searched for three days but did not find him. When they returned to Elisha, who was staying in Jericho, he said to them, "Didn't I tell you not to go?" (2 Kings 2:11–18 NIV)

What are you waiting for? Are you ready for what God has in store next?

This almost six-week journey has been preparing us for what God is leading us to. From this point on, we must pay attention to two things:

1. We continue to deepen and develop our relationship with God, trusting him more each day.
2. We cling to the promises of God for our strength in this journey.

Notice what Elisha did. When he saw the chariot of fire, he tried to stay close to Elijah, but he didn't want Elijah to go. Why? I think he may have felt there was more to learn, more to do. But when God tells you it's time to step out in faith, be ready to follow through.

Discernment has to be a journey like the one we've been on. This may seem like a long time to wait, but it is better if we allow God to shape and mold us before we do anything. I pray that during this time, you have experienced a deep peace about the decision you needed to make. I also hope and pray you will walk out with more confidence and in the strength of the Lord into your next step.

The internal work still is not complete. I hope you'll continue to foster the habit of reading scripture and seeking God daily so you can grow in faith and in his knowledge.

May the grace of our Lord, Jesus Christ, strengthen you for your journey ahead. Just watch God do his work in and through you.

Receive this charge to live a life of victory in the decision. Church, always go in the peace, power, and *victory* of Jesus Christ, today and always. Go in his peace. Amen.

Let's pray: Lord Jesus, guide me, and reveal yourself and your direction to me.

WESLEY COVENANT PRAYER

I am no longer my own, but yours.
Put me to what you will,
rank me with whom you will;
put me to doing,
put me to suffering;
let me be employed for you,
or laid aside for you,
exalted for you,
or brought low for you;
let me be full, let me be empty,
let me have all things,
let me have nothing:
I freely and wholeheartedly yield all things
to your pleasure and disposal.
And now, glorious and blessed God,
Father, Son and Holy Spirit,
you are mine and I am yours.
So be it.
And the covenant now made on earth,
let it be ratified in heaven.
Amen.

DAILY REFLECTION

Write about what God has revealed about himself. How is it with your soul, just sitting in the presence of God? What is going through your mind and heart about the decision or choice you need to make?

> The people of the city said to Elisha, "Look, our Lord, this town is well situated, as you can see, but the water is bad and the land is unproductive." "Bring me a new bowl," he said, "and put salt in it." So they brought it to him. Then he went out to the spring and threw the salt into it, saying, "This is what the Lord says: 'I have healed this water. Never again will it cause death or make the land unproductive.'" And the water has remained pure to this day, according to the word Elisha had spoken." (2 Kings 2:19–22 NIV)

I love the last phase of this passage: "the water has remained pure to this day." This is what we are hoping and living for. We live in the hope that Jesus Christ is making us holy, whole, complete, *and* pure.

Our lives are books that other people read. What story does your life tell? Is your life an example of who Jesus is and why others should follow him? This doesn't mean you live perfectly; you're human, and you will make mistakes. This does mean, however, that you have opportunities to show how you have been transformed.

Look at Elisha. Because of his trust, perseverance, and faith, God made him a mighty prophet in Israel. The people began to look up to Elisha because he was willing to give the truth about the Lord.

I pray the same can be said about you and me.

This has been a journey to help you sit in the presence of God, seek God's guidance, and decide what you should do. How has this journey been for you?

As you step out in faith for your next steps, I pray that God works mightily in you, and other people can come to know the living

God, who is working in and through you. I pray you continually take time to seek God daily and trust him to provide for your daily needs.

I pray you can find ways to praise and trust God for who he is and what he is doing in your life and in this world.

> May the grace of the Lord Jesus Christ, and the love of God, and the fellowship of the Holy Spirit be with you all. (2 Corinthians 13:14 NIV)

Amen.

Let's pray: Lord Jesus, guide me, and reveal yourself and your direction to me.

WESLEY COVENANT PRAYER

I am no longer my own, but yours.
Put me to what you will,
rank me with whom you will;
put me to doing,
put me to suffering;
let me be employed for you,
or laid aside for you,
exalted for you,
or brought low for you;
let me be full, let me be empty,
let me have all things,
let me have nothing:
I freely and wholeheartedly yield all things
to your pleasure and disposal.
And now, glorious and blessed God,
Father, Son and Holy Spirit,
you are mine and I am yours.
So be it.

And the covenant now made on earth,
let it be ratified in heaven.
Amen.

DAILY REFLECTION

Write about what God has revealed about himself. How is it with your soul, just sitting in the presence of God? What is going through your mind and heart about the decision or choice you need to make?

END OF FORTY-DAY REFLECTIONS

Today is a day of Sabbath rest. Use this day to connect with and praise God, and reflect on how you have experienced God in this past week and during this six-week time of discernment.

Read: Psalm 98

Reflect: How have you experienced God's grace in this past week? How has this period of forty days impacted you and your relationship with God and his people?

Let's pray: Lord Jesus, guide me, and reveal yourself and your direction to me.

WESLEY COVENANT PRAYER

I am no longer my own, but yours.
Put me to what you will,
rank me with whom you will;
put me to doing,
put me to suffering;
let me be employed for you,
or laid aside for you,
exalted for you,
or brought low for you;
let me be full, let me be empty,
let me have all things,
let me have nothing:
I freely and wholeheartedly yield all things
to your pleasure and disposal.
And now, glorious and blessed God,
Father, Son and Holy Spirit,

you are mine and I am yours.
So be it.
And the covenant now made on earth,
let it be ratified in heaven.
Amen.

NEXT STEPS

I am excited for what God has in store for you. I am excited for how God is working in and through you. There may have been days when you wanted to quit or to move that you thought was right about the decision or choice. I am praying God has blessed you with the direction to move. If you are still unsure, it could be that God is trying to get your attention a little more, or this may not be the right time to make the decision or choice. No matter what happens, know that God is with you and is working in and through you in every step of your journey of life.

This journey has been a gift for me. As I was going through a particular discernment process, these are the devotionals I wrote and reflected upon. Writing these every day was not always easy, nor was it what I really *wanted* to do, but I am so grateful for the intentional time spent with the presence of the living God. I am grateful for the time spent in the life and ministry of Elijah and Elisha.

Now it's your turn to live out the life that God has called for you. Are you ready to step out in faith and trust that the best and right decision has been made? Do you believe you'll be the person God desires you to be in your decision? Do you believe who God is and who God says he is? Do you believe who God says you are?

The kingdom of God is known through the life you live. Find time to praise God and thank him for this journey.

I would love to hear about your journey! Feel free to contact me through my website: www.revryanstratton.com.

In Christ,

Ryan Stratton

APPENDIX

WHO DOES GOD SAY YOU ARE?

Throughout this journey, we have asked the questions that deal with who God says you are and what kind of person you want to be. The following is an essay I wrote in one of my seminary classes that may help to understand what it means to be *made in the image of God*—in other words, who God says you are and what kind of person you want to be.

Created in the Image of God

> In the beginning God created the heavens and the earth ... Then God said, 'Let us make mankind in our image, in our likeness ... So God created mankind in his own image, in the image of God he created them; male and female he created them.[5]

The imago Dei has been a doctrine of debate for many years.

> Theological anthropological claims were derived by applying the general account of creatureliness to human creatures in particular, qualified by the claim that what distinguishes them as specifically human is that God creates them into the image of God.[6]

Throughout the centuries, people have been in many discussions and studies about what it means to be made in God's image. There

---

[5] Genesis 1:1, 26–27 New International Version.
[6] J. B. Webster. *The Oxford Handbook of Systematic Theology*, 122.

are many theories from being made in the image of love, to being a good and moral person, to having the creative ability to steward and care for the earth, to … I'm sure many other ideas. All of which point to the character and personhood of God. Just what is the image of God? What does this mean for humankind and its identity? What are the implications for salvation and life everlasting?

For a while, I have fallen into the camp of saying God is love, and we are created in the image of love, but I have come to better understand this is true, yet not a complete understanding. Why? Because of the way love is defined in our current culture—more dealing with feelings than as a way of life. Another way I have understood the image of God is we have morality within us. It is true humanity has the moral law written on our hearts. This is why we can determine what is right and what is wrong. Duane Stephen Long writes, "The moral life has its origin in our creation in the image of God and its end in our restoration and return to that image."[7] But I have some reservations about this. Is the imago Dei "just" about morality? Are we not considered moral when we move on from this life? Or does morality take on a new meaning or dimension when we transition into the next life?

Now we come to what I think is the real issue—who is God, and what is God like? I also believe that how we live our lives shows what we believe about the nature and person of God within us. When we take the time to study, reflect on, and pray about who and what we are, we can begin to understand our purpose in this world because we understand there is a deep level to goodness within the world and within the nature and character of God.

> The triune God is complete goodness…the triune
> God is the perfect fullness of being…God loves his
> own goodness such that he seeks to share it. This

---

[7] Ibid., 460.

occurs through the second person of the Trinity, who is the image of God.[8]

Our entire lives should point and be directed to the Son, the second person of the Trinity, Jesus Christ, to best understand the image of God.

To this end, I am concluding the image of God is about relationship. To be made in God's image shows we can have a deep relationship with the Creator, other people, ourselves, and creation. One of the things to understand is that God is in relationship with Godself through the Trinity. The Trinity, the relationship with the Father, the Son, and the Holy Spirit, show us it is possible to live in perfect harmony and peace with others. I believe this is God's intent—we live, with the Spirit of God dwelling with us, in perfect harmony and peace with everyone and everything around us while we take care of and tend to the created order, as God would do here, since we are the image-bearers of God and are God's representatives here on earth. As Stephen Fowl writes,

> In creation God freely wills not simply the existence of humans created in the image of God, but God also desires fellowship with humans, offering them a share in the divine life. This is both the intention with which God created and the end for which God created.[9]

And everything was all well and good until free will got the best of humans, and the divine image within humanity became marred through the entry of sin and evil in our world.

---

[8] Ibid.
[9] Ibid., 348.

IMAGE OF GOD BROKEN WITHIN US

Humanity was created to be God's image-bearers on earth and take care of the created order.

> The issue at stake, rather, is the theological account of the specific relationship of two causalities to each other—the triune God, creator and redeemer, and the human being, created in the image of God and existing under the condition of sin."[10] Now that we understand this concept, we have to take responsibility and respond to God. We can either accept gratefully this image and task, or we can reject it. When we reject God, this response, "may take the form of efforts 'to be self-constituting and isolated being', i.e. the form of sin that distorts the image of God vertically and horizontally.[11]

Because of sin, we easily lose our divine purpose within us and end up making ourselves into the image of anything else that makes us happy. Thus, idolatry, greed, murder, thievery, adultery, etc., become the "gods" we seek to fulfill us, and we have allowed these other "gods" to lead us to live for us, rather than the life God created for us. We continue to mar the image of God within us by reshaping our lives by the relationship(s) we have with other entities, which we feel are more valuable than the life of God within us. We miss out on living the divine relationship of the Trinity in which we have been created. Why? "Sin obtains, with the consequence that the entire relations that constitute persons is distorted or 'fallen,'"[12] meaning we have lost our way, our purpose, and our identity. Unfortunately, because the reality of sin and evil has entered into our world and

---

[10] Ibid., 291.

[11] Ibid., 132.

[12] Ibid.

every human, there is nothing we can do, on our own, to change our relationship with God and restore us to the divine image.

What happens next is humanity will begin to seek after other things, people, or statuses to believe they have found who they are and what their purpose is for life. Idols and idolatry now come into view, which distorts the vision humans have of themselves and the created order even more. We think we can "fix" this problem on our own, so we will do everything possible to try to "earn" God's favor and acceptance, but we can end up making things worse because our focus is not on God but on ourselves and how we want God to fix us so our lives are better. It is too easy to treat God as our magic genie and expect God to do our bidding, thus attempting to make God an idol who works for us. We need the grace of God. We need God to do something, to intervene in our lives to make this change for us. We need God to remind us of who we are and replace the image of ourselves once again with the divine image to restore all relationships in this world.

GOD REVEALS HIMSELF

Due to the fall (sin and evil becoming attached to human life and existence), humanity had lost so much of its identity concerning how to be in relationship with God, others, self, and creation that is it impossible for us to restore the relationship status we were created in without any assistance. Therefore, God sent the Son, Jesus the Christ, as the one who would save and atone for the sins of the world. What this means is that God descended from heaven to show the people of Israel (eventually, the world) what it means to be human and live into the divine image. To best reveal himself to the world, God sent Jesus, the human revelation of God in flesh. Jesus is the way we can experience a restored relationship with God, others, self, and creation.

Before Jesus came, humanity did not have a full revelation about who God is and what God's nature is like because God revealed small amounts of the divine character at different points in history (see Noah, Abraham, Moses, David, the prophets). Humanity was not able to grasp the richness and deepness of God, so God needed to send a full representation of himself to show the world who he is and what his character is like. Jesus is this revelation for humanity. In Colossians 1:15, the apostle writes a hymn and confession of faith that was used to teach about who Jesus is: "The Son is the image of the invisible God, the firstborn over all creation."[13] The revelation of God has been made known through Jesus the Christ. Without Jesus, God would still be unknowable in the manner we can know God today. Therefore, humanity would not know the divine image given to humanity at creation. It is also through the Holy Spirit within us that we can more fully understand who we are because of the image of God, by leading us to Jesus Christ.

> The gift of the Holy Spirit invites us to participate
> in the life of God by drawing us into the life of the
> Son.[14]

MADE IN THE IMAGE OF CHRIST

> As a human person who is the image of the invisible
> God, Jesus Christ is not merely a spirit or soul but
> an embodied human being.[15]

Jesus is the way humanity can personally know God—who God is, what the character of God is like, and thus, who we are as people.

---

[13] New International Version.

[14] Webster, *The Oxford Handbook of Systematic Theology*, 460.

[15] Ibid., 75.

To know who God is, the theological virtue of faith is necessary.[16]

To be restored to the image of God, God allowed humanity to have faith in God's Son, Jesus the Christ.

Everyone who believes that Jesus is the Christ is born of God ...[17]

Jesus tells his disciple Phillip, "Anyone who has seen me has seen the Father."[18] To know Jesus is to know God. To know God is to know who God is. To know who God is reveals who we are. To know who we are reveals the divine nature within us. To know the divine nature within us reveals how we should live, in relationship with God, other people, ourselves, and even the created order.

Jesus has been made known to the world, and now humanity can know what it means to be made into the image of God by being recreated and reformed into the image of Christ because of God's grace. Through our faith, we direct back to God through Jesus the Christ. The image of Christ does everything possible to proclaim and connect the world with the already-yet-coming kingdom of God. We can see how this is carried out within the pages of the New Testament.

In the New Testament the imago is identified with Jesus...the imago was not fulfilled at creation but rather is a divinely given eschatological destiny. This destiny is fulfilled by the eschatological Spirit, who, transforming human beings by incorporating them

---

[16] Ibid., 460.
[17] 1 John 5:1 New International Version.
[18] John 14:9 New International Version.

'in Christ' ... drawing them into participation in the divine life.[19]

One of the ways we can see this lived out and practiced is in the letters of Paul to the people at Corinth. He writes, "Follow [imitate me] my example, as I follow [imitate] the example of Christ."[20] To fully live into the divine image, we (humanity) need to follow the example of and imitate the life of Jesus. It is in Jesus Christ that the image of God is fully lived out. We, humanity, now have the chance to display and live into love, morality, joy, peaceful relationships, etc., because this is all part of the divine image, the imago Dei. This is all possible by placing and grounding our faith in Jesus Christ.

Faith in Christ is where this transformation begins.

> Persons are re-created, the image of God restored, when they are conformed to Christ.[21]

> The theological virtues, gifts, and beatitudes restore us into the image of God, Christ, whose life is the foundation for this restoration. Through his incarnation and its meditation through the church in word and sacrament, we participate in his righteousness.[22]

This kind of life leads us to the gift of salvation and understanding how we should live in this life and in the life to come.

---

[19] Webster, *The Oxford Handbook of Systematic Theology*, 129.
[20] 1 Corinthians 11:1 New International Version.
[21] Webster, *The Oxford Handbook of Systematic Theology*, 132.
[22] Ibid., 461.

SALVATION AND THE GOAL OF SALVATION

For people to fully realize a life lived in and with the imago Dei, humanity needs to be recreated into the original image God intended. Nothing will be set right; no relationship will ever be peaceful or just until the imago Dei is fully restored in the life of the follower of Christ. This begins a process of being recreated, being made new in Christ. The process of being made new, being recreated, does not take away our uniqueness; it simply means the essence of who we are (our motives and focus in this world) will be recreated and recentered around the God, who created us.

> Re-created persons truly image God. Thus personhood is inherently centered outside itself. Since, as created, personhood is already intrinsically related to God, God's relating to re-create does not threaten person's autonomy and subjectivity.[23]

All of this is made possible through the work of Jesus Christ. As the apostle Paul reminded the people of Corinth, "If anyone is in Christ, the new creation has come. The old is gone, the new is here!"[24] Humanity can and will be recreated into something new, something that God intends, something that will allow humanity to dwell and live with God in life everlasting, or as N. T. Wright says, "life after life." This is the goal of salvation—theosis.

> Theosis (divinization) is not, of course, a 'becoming God', but being made into the 'likeness' of God, which means being drawn much more deeply into the relationships in which God exists as a Trinity of

---

[23] Ibid., 132.
[24] 2 Corinthians 5:17 New International Version.

love ... salvation is a 'coming closer to God' or an 'ever intensifying relationship.'[25]

What this means is humanity moves closer and closer to the original design of perfect relationships whole, at the same time moving away from the relationship and damage of a life guided and lived under the curse of sin.

One of the beautiful aspects of salvation is the past, present, and future aspects of the working of God in our lives. We have been saved. We are saved. We will be saved. God's act of salvation is constantly moving us closer and closer to the divine and deeper and deeper into the divine relationship. With each act of God, we realize more and more of the divine image within us, and we can see how God, because of the work of Jesus Christ and the activity of the Holy Spirit, is moving us to live into more of the divine image. Forgiveness of the sin nature within us is transforming the marred part of us and transforming the sin nature back into the imago Dei.

WHAT DOES THIS MEAN?

Restoring the divine image within us, transforming us into the image of Christ, means God is making us whole. We will not have to think there is something we're missing out on because we find our completeness in the presence of God. After all, we will find God's image within us and working through us. It is our relationship with God that makes us whole. Being whole means we see how we are set apart—made holy. This is the goal of reclaiming the imago Dei in us. We become a set-apart people shining forth God's light, love, and character into the world. We live into the Great Commission (going, teaching, baptizing, making disciples) because this is who we were created to be and because we have a deep longing for others to know, realize, and live into the divine image within themselves too.

[25] Webster, *The Oxford Handbook of Systematic Theology*, 176.

How cool is it? God gave us the Holy Spirit to know God personally and to know God is guiding, directing, encouraging us each step of the way to not forsake or quench the Spirit within us, but to become more and more into the likeness and image of Jesus Christ. This is the image the world needs today and what the world needs to see so transformation can take place, and we can visibly witness the kingdom of God reigning and ruling in this world. We become, by the grace of God, new creatures, transformed into whole and holy people, doing the work and living the life God originally intended for God's people.

Sources Consulted
Webster, J. B., Katherine Tanner, and Iain Torrance. *The Oxford Handbook of Systematic Theology*. Oxford, New York: Oxford University Press, 2007.

NEW AND UNIQUE PRAYER JOURNAL

You know what a gift it is to have someone pray for you. You also know how powerful it is to pray for another person.

Have you ever considered giving someone a journal of the prayers that you prayed for them?

When we pray for others, we help others experience God's incredible presence. This is the perfect prayer journal for you! Record your prayers, and watch the presence of God move in and through your life, as well as the person for whom you prayed these prayers. This journal is a perfect way to record the prayers you've prayed for your child, spouse, or friend. You can use this guide to write down your prayers. There is also space for the recipient to record his or her own prayers, as well as to record answers to prayer.

Think of the impact your written prayers will have on the person receiving them!

Order your copy at www.revryanstratton.com.

Printed in the United States
by Baker & Taylor Publisher Services